The Sol Plaatje European Union
Poetry Anthology

Vol VIII

The Sol Plaatje European Union Poetry Anthology

Volume VIII

Selected by Rustum Kozain, Goodenough Mashego, Pieter Odendaal, Makhosazana Xaba, Mongane Wally Serote

The views and opinions expressed in this publication are not necessarily those of the funder.

First published by Jacana Media (Pty) Ltd in 2018

10 Orange Street
Sunnyside
Auckland Park 2092
South Africa
+2711 628 3200
www.jacana.co.za

© Individual contributors, 2018
© Cover photograph: Ruth Simbao. Athi-Patra Ruga, The Future White Woman of Azania, 2012, performed for the exhibition "Making Way: Contemporary Art from South Africa and China", curated by Ruth Simbao.

All rights reserved.

ISBN 978-1-4314-2721-5

Cover design by Shawn Paikin
Editing by Linda Da Nova
Proofreading by Megan Mance
Set in Ehrhardt 11/13pt
Printed by CTP Printers, Cape Town
Job no. 003382

See a complete list of Jacana titles at www.jacana.co.za

Contents

Foreword xi
A message from the sponsor, *The European Union* xix
A note on translation, *Innocentia Mhlambi* xxi
ISIXHOSA, *Zukiswa Muriel Adonis* 1
    THE XHOSA LANGUAGE, *an English translation by*
    Angelinah Dazela 4
THE ATTACK OF THE PESTS, *Jim Pascual Agustin* 6
HONDEDROLLE OP DIE GRASPERK, *Du Toit Albertze* 7
    DOG SHIT ON THE LAWN, *an English translation by*
    Pieter Odendaal 8
BRAAI, *Du Toit Albertze* 9
    BRAAI, *an English translation by Pieter Odendaal* 12
THERE IS, *Kyle Allan* 15
JUST THE LYNTJIE, *Mia Arderne* 16
NSATI WA MAKARATA, *Vonani Bila* 17
    A WIFE THAT PLAYS CARDS, *an English translation by*
    Aubrey Neo Sehlahla 22
BONTEHEUWEL, *René Bohnen* 27
    BONTEHEUWEL, *an English translation by René Bohnen* 28
THE THIRST, *Christine Coates* 29
IKAGENG, *Christine Coates* 30
ULWANDLE, *Silulundi Coki* 32
    THE SEA, *an English translation by Angelinah Dazela* 33
KANTI NIYAHLUPHA!, *Silulundi Coki* 34
    YOU BRING DISCOMFORT, *an English translation by*
    Angelinah Dazela 35
IINWELE, *Silulundi Coki* 36
    THE HAIR, *an English translation by Angelinah Dazela* 38

MONT AUX SOURCES – THE LIGHTNING, *Mark de Wet* .. 40
DELAYED OBITUARY, *Luthando Dlamini* 41
(AUSCHWITZ)-BIRKENAU 2 SHOE, *Ruth Everson* 42
NAMHLANJE NDIVULELE IHAGU ESITIYENI SIKA
    TATA, *Nobuntu Gantana* 43
    A PIG IN THE GARDEN, *an English translation by*
    Angelinah Dazela.. 44
TRIGGER WARNING SERIES, *Sarah Godsell* 45
PLEIADES, *Richard Higgs* 47
SAL NOOIT 'N WITMAN DATE NIE, *Veronique Jephtas* 49
    WILL NEVER DATE A WHITE MAN, *an English translation*
    by Pieter Odendaal.. 50
NGENZE NAMI NGIZIGQAJE, *Zandile Khumalo* 51
    MAKE ME PROUD OF MYSELF, *an English translation by*
    Dr Innocentia Jabulisile Mhlambi 53
FATSHE LAKA KGUTLELA HAE, *Thabiso Tsietsi Lakajoe* 55
    MAYIBUYE, *an English translation by Goodenough Mashego* 57
O MPHOQILE KE O TSHEPILE, *George Thabiso Leseba* 59
    YOU BETRAYED MY TRUST, *an English translation by*
    Goodenough Mashego 63
ESCAPE, *Busisiwe Mahlangu*.. 67
SCRAPS, *Busisiwe Mahlangu*.. 68
PHELO BJA LEHONO, *Tshepiso Makgoloane* 70
    IN LIFE TODAY, *an English translation by Goodenough Mashego* 72
BOKAMOSO BJA AFRIKA-BORWA, *Tshepiso Makgoloane* 74
    SOUTH AFRICA'S FUTURE, *an English translation by*
    Goodenough Mashego 76
ISIBELETHO, *Mbali Malimela* 78
    THE WOMB, *an English translation by Dr Innocentia Jabulisile*
    Mhlambi 80

NGIYAPHICA PHICA, *Mbali Malimela* 82
    I HAVE A RIDDLE AND MY RIDDLE IS, *an English translation by Dr Innocentia Jabulisile Mhlambi* 83
SLEEPLESS IN SOWETO, *Anga Mamfanya* 84
CANCER, *Sibulelo Manamatela* 86
IF WE WERE FOR SALE, *Tshedza Mashamba* 87
NGIYANILIBALELA, *Bongani Masilela* 89
    I FORGIVE YOU, *an English translation by Dr Sponono Katjie Mahlangu* 90
NNAHANELE, *Aaron Mpho Masowa* 91
    GIVE ME SOME THOUGHT, *an English translation by Goodenough Mashego* 93
UMAKULINGANWE, *Zongezile Matshoba* 95
    EQUALITY, *an English translation by Angelinah Dazela* 96
UNGALONKULU, *Zongezile Matshoba* 97
    THE HEFTY FIGHTER, *an English translation by Angelinah Dazela* 98
BA FOFILE, *Katise Mawela* 99
    THEY'RE GONE, *an English translation by Goodenough Mashego* 100
SONDAE MIDDAE, *Marthe McLoud* 101
    SUNDAY AFTERNOONS, *an English translation by Pieter Odendaal* 102
EVEREST, *Janine Milne* 103
HA RE ESO FIHLE, *Thabiso Mofokeng* 104
    WE ARE NOT THERE YET, *an English translation by Goodenough Mashego* 106
BOMENETŠA, *Daniel Matsepe Mohlala* 109
    DISHONESTY, *an English translation by Goodenough Mashego* .111
MEGOKGO YA LEFASE, *Daniel Matsepe Mohlala* 113
    TEARS OF THE WORLD, *an English translation by Goodenough Mashego* 114

EAT AROUND THE ROT, *Dikeledi Mokoena* 115
THE BRIDGE, *Mjele Msimang* 116
THE THINGS I FOUND IN THE FIRE, *Mjele Msimang* 117
NDZIMA N'WANANGA, *Moses Mtileni* 118
    NDZIMA, MY CHILD, *an English translation by Aubrey Neo Sehlahla* 120
MKHOHLISI, *Sifiso Mtshali* 122
    DECEIVER, *an English translation by Dr Innocentia Jabulisile Mhlambi* 124
BLACK OPHELIAS, *Sinaso Mxakaza* 126
DURBAN, 1986, *Pamela Newham* 127
LITTLE LOVE LETTER, *Sandile Ngidi* 128
BHEKI MSELEKU REGRETS YOU, *Bomikazi Njoloza* 129
STHANDWA SAM AFRIKA, *Simphiwe Nolutshungu* 131
    DEAREST AFRICA!, *an English translation by Angelinah Dazela* 133
A SCENE AT GROOTE SCHUUR RES, *Zola Nongogo* 135
UNISA, *Sipho Albert Ntombela* 136
    UNISA, *an English translation by Dr Innocentia Jabulisile Mhlambi* 138
MINA NGIYADIDEKA, *Sipho Albert Ntombela* 140
    I AM CONFUSED, *an English translation by Dr Innocentia Jabulisile Mhlambi* 141
LUFUNO A SI TSERERE, *Mushayathoni Bridget Nwovhe* 143
    LOVE IS NOT EASY, *an English translation by Aubrey Neo Sehlahla* 145
HONDSEGEDAGTE, *Hans Pienaar* 147
    DOG THOUGHTS, *an English translation by Pieter Odendaal* 148
BATJHA, *Sehloho Piet Rampai* 149
    GENERATION X, *an English translation by Goodenough Mashego* 151

LABELS, *Juliette Rose-Innes* 153
FAITH, *Deborah Seddon* 154
O SWELE MPHATO, *Moses Seletisha* 156
    THE INITIATION SCHOOL WENT UP IN FLAMES,
    an English translation by Goodenough Mashego 158
HAZARDS, *Nkwana Joshua Serutle* 160
OBAB' ABANGEBABA, *Bukelani Mmelly Shangase* 161
    FATHERS WHO ARE NOT FATHERS, *an English*
    translation by Dr Innocentia Jabulisile Mhlambi 164
KONAKELEPHI?, *Bukelani Mmelly Shangase* 167
    WHERE DID IT GO WRONG?, *an English translation by*
    Dr Innocentia Jabulisile Mhlambi 168
IZIZUKULWANE, *Bukelani Mmelly Shangase* 169
    GENERATIONS, *Dr Innocentia Jabulisile Mhlambi* 171
INDULI YEXHWAYELO, *Siwaphiwe Fortune Shweni* 173
    THE HILL OF AGONY, *an English translation by Angelinah*
    Dazela 175
ANINA, *Francine Simon* 177
DEEPA, *Francine Simon* 179
NTWA YA BANA BA THARI, *Tiisetso Thiba* 180
    CIVIL WAR, *an English translation by Goodenough Mashego* 182
FREEDOM, *Elizabeth Trew* 184
LIKE SILHOUETTES (AFTER FATHERLESS KIDS),
    Thato Tshukudu 185
INNOCENT, *Elna van Niekerk* 187
    INNOCENT, *an English translation by Pieter Odendaal* 189
BELHAR, *Elna van Niekerk* 191
    BELHAR, *an English translation by Pieter Odendaal* 194
DIE OVERALL VAN MY, *Lester Walbrugh* 197
    THIS OVERALL OF MINE, *an English translation by Pieter*
    Odendaal 199

CITY DUMP, *Jeannie Wallace McKeown* 201
ACCUMULATED GRIEF, *Crystal Warren* 202
DETAILS OF DEATH, *Crystal Warren* 203
STATE OF THE NATION, *Crystal Warren* 204
IMMIGRANT, *Flow Wellington* 206
APOLLONIAN TRICK, *Athol Williams* 207
Biographies. 209
What is the European Union (EU)? 227

Foreword

After reading through the 30 poems, I asked myself: What is poetry? What is a poet? Then I did not want to write what I have just written. I wished I had not asked these questions. This is because the questions have a serious meaning – they may be asking: "… who is looting who …?" This is what they may be asking. There is something of that in the poems. But this is because there is also something else after a closer scrutiny. The poems are written in two languages: one is original and the other is a translation. Those languages are cultured from different histories even though they are only languages. When the finesse of the language is drowned and has disappeared because it cannot breathe, what then is left of the poem? There is a skilled, thin, but acutely present quietness and simplicity that fights the violence and force of the surgeon's-scalpel handling of translations, as the languages are juxtaposed. Of course, that depends on the skill of the surgeon.

In the foreword I did for the *Sol Plaatjie European Union Poetry Anthology Volume VII*, after I read the poems in that volume, over and over, I was extremely happy when I wrote 'South Africa is a poem'.

In this volume (Volume VIII) the poems are typically South African. There is nothing in them that we do not know about us as South Africans. In that regard, they are very accurate. The poems have penetrated the South African heart, feelings and statistics – the one plus one is two of South Africa, plus its mystery, beauty and insanity. They are on the dot with them. The poems, because the poets who wrote them use their poetic licence, penetrate quickly and let the tears or blood flow or the hurt settle in life because life has taught the poets something. The poets are as accurate as science can be – however, the poets know about dreams and therefore they also know nightmares; they attest that human beings do not live by science only, as some would like us to believe. That is not to undermine science when I say this; I am merely saying there is something called feelings in life!

...

She eyed me with those extra white eyes
She cleared her throat and then she said
"My name is Ntombenhle, The Beautiful one
I am a daughter of Sokhela
I am of the Mkhize clan from eMakhabeleni
Here in Johannesburg, I survive through selling my body."
I was tongue-tied; what I said next made and did not make sense
Even though there was a nagging idea that I should stay away from here,
I was embarrassed to do so! I stood motionless!

...

"...I will never be a maiden
Even though I can wish it with all my heart
You are only seeing an image of a maiden
My maidenhood was taken away from me by fathers
Fathers who were not fathers because they lacked integrity
Fathers who were in love with my mother raped me repeatedly."

...

Poems do rhyme. Poems have rhythm. Poems can break logic and break the usual rules as they fetch feelings from the depth of the issues facing and challenging the poet. But here also, the English language is being taught isiZulu – African culture. The African culture which is as a result of African history is vastly different from that of the English which is also as a result of English history. The incidences may be the same, in the same way also, human culture is the same, because human history can also be the same. That is why poetry, when the poets attempt to fathom everything human, is complex with simplicity.

You cannot force love because if you do, it will kill you. ('Love is Not Easy', the poet calls the poem.)

It is like saying love, to love, is very dangerous. Which human being does not know this? Because it is a universal human experience, in other words, because love is for all human beings; its twists and turns are familiar to all humans, perhaps even to all animals – hear the cry of a cat that is in love, and tell us what you have heard!

If there are many and different, but also similar, references in the environment of the human race, then we shall, from our instinct and also from being educated, know we will know the same things. This is what the first and the second languages say, but the languages will also come to a halt. Ntombenhle is not The Beautiful one, but a beautiful maiden. These are subtleties, slight differences, at times meaningless, at times so important like Beautiful one and beautiful maiden referring to the woman whose life we are reading about in the poem, when she tells us about her values, but also lack of values because of her life experiences insofar as the nation would judge her. A matter she knows very well as it could also be an un-healing wound until she lies prostrate in a box of wood, motionless, never having been the apple of the eye of her village, township and her family. It is a poet who pens such feelings, which have been experienced and left whatever behind, on the being of those who experienced them.

There is that with the poets. They ask you to seek and search because they do not want these busy people from villages, townships or suburbs to forget that at times what they are busy with results in such things where girls will never become maidens – nonsense like that sentencing the little girls and little boys to death while being alive.

> ...
> *It is my talk about love to her that dug up wounds in*
>   *the young lady*
> *The conversation was disrupted when a flashy car*
>   *stopped by*
> *It stopped and then the driver's window was opened*
> *The lady took one look and bid me farewell*
> *And said, "I bid you to go, this is my client that has*
>   *just stopped."*
> *I did not know whether I had to bid her farewell too*
> *I stood fixed at a spot as I looked on as the flashy car*
> *slowly drove away*
> *After a long pause I heard myself talking alone like a*
>   *mad man*
> *"Everything that happens, do so because of a reason."*
> ...

The poet suggests in this poem that both the girl and the boy of this village, of this township, of this suburb, were wounded. Quietly the poet wonders as to what will happen to either. What is the future for both? The poet hopes that the villagers, the township and the suburb dwellers will not leave the matter there, just like that, but that they will remember that an unexamined life is not worth living!

What is it with men and women and sexuality? What is it that they must learn so that they know what to do with this thing? Religion does not know. Science does not know. Culture does not know. It is easy to judge. It is easy to blame, if we remember that sexuality can be a very wild beast! It is created to be insatiable. We know that the word is *restrain*. What is that faced with a beast? How and what must we learn about that word – so that the little boys and little girls can be nurtured to know and love each other?

Here is another poem:

...

I am confused
we are going forward, we are going backward
We are going to Canaan, we are going to Egypt
In Egypt it was like this
In Canaan it is this
Where is the difference?

...

I am confused
Where is the Government of the people?
Where is the will of the people?
Where are the leaders of the people?
No, I am not referring to the window dressers
The lives of the people are at stake
...

The people and their governments. What is that? Where is that? What does it do?

The poet says:

...
Here is a tyre running away with fire.
Here is a crossfire of rubber bullets
Here is the smoke from stun grenades
...

Where has the government not gone wild and mad? Fire. Bullets. Grenades. Which government does not own these and has not used them against its nationals?

For 15 years the people and the government in South Africa spoke to each other – not that there were never moments of what one poet called 'Mahlalerwa' (wild dogs). There were. There will be. Goodenough Mashego, one of whose tasks now and then is translation of poems, elaborated on this concept:

"... First and foremost 'lehlarelwa' is a wild dog in the family of wolves, jackals, etc. They are those beasts that hunt in packs and usually take advantage of either weak animals or leftovers from other beasts' kills. The poet uses this word as a metaphor for a group of criminals who prowl the streets in search for their victim. In the poem (which was being reviewed then) 'Mahlalerwa' is a plural of 'Lehlalerwa'. So he pluralises it to give it the right animal impact ..."

The poem 'Mahlalerwa' "... is about the rape of an unknown woman in the belly of the night by a group of young men. She gets spotted as she comes home from work. The pack of men escort her until a window opens and they overpower and gang rape her. In the last stanza the poet then changes tack and takes a political stance where he says after they violated the woman, the wolf pack started making political statements, toyi-toying for the case to disappear ..."

If the woman becomes a good government and

Mahlalerwa are coup perpetrators we can look at the poem 'I Am Confused' – and we must ask the question of what must be done so that the people are never confused by populists, liars, plotters, terrorists and opportunists, especially on the African continent which was once a playing ground for coup perpetrators.

...
I am confused
Where is the Government of the people?
Where is the will of the people?
Where are the leaders of the people?
No, I am not referring to the window dressers
The lives of the people are at stake
...

With rhythm and rhyming lines and with utter simplicity of expression on the surface, the poet raises very complex political concepts. What must be the relationship between the people and their governments, to prevent coups? What should the people know for them to know when the government is under attack by Mahlalerwa? What must be the responsibility of government to ensure that while it protects and defends democratic principles and the constitution of the land, the people know that there are other activities "... in the belly of the night ..."? How do the people become the eyes and the ears of themselves, of their country, and how do they protect what they value most – their freedom?

Mongane Wally Serote
August 2018

A message from the sponsor

The Sol Plaatje European Union Poetry Award and Anthology, since their establishment some nine years ago, have become part of South Africa's colourful cultural fabric and heritage. They have reflected joy and achievement, gloom and despair, and in this have provided a mirror to, as well as have become part of, the challenging path towards the building of the South African nation.

As I pen these words on 18 July 2018 – Mandela Day on the centenary of the great statesman's birth – I consider it appropriate to reflect on elements of this difficult journey.

I suspect that it would be fairly accurate to state that the editor, author, translator, eventual politician and towering intellectual, Solomon Tshekisho Plaatje – to whom this wonderful poetry initiative is dedicated – dreamed of an inclusive, united South Africa with values based on equality and justice. As a founding member of the South African Native National Congress, his vision of a common South Africa under the rule of law meant overcoming, most notably, racial segregation and domination by one race group over another. Plaatje died in 1932, some 62 years before Nelson Rolihlahla Mandela became South Africa's first democratically elected president.

By celebrating what President Mandela stood for, as we do today, it would surely not be far-fetched to assert that in so doing, across the world, we also celebrate what Plaatje stood for. Both men sought to set South Africa on a course towards humanity and nation building.

And so, back to the poetry award and anthology: I believe that this multilingual initiative has and will continue to play its part in the evolution of the South African identity. Inspired by the multilingualism within the European Union, it seemed only natural that the EU Delegation to South Africa would again, in this European Year of Cultural Heritage, wish to support the Sol Plaatje European Union Poetry Award and Anthology.

In the past few months its winning poets have participated in workshops and festivals in various parts of South Africa. It is wonderful to be associated with this success story ... it is not uncommon to meet people who, when told about the competition, are quick to point out that they, in fact, have acquired one or more of the anthologies.

I conclude by thanking all involved in making this dynamic initiative the success it has become and look forward to reading this eighth volume of what has now grown into a small library of Sol Plaatje European Union Poetry anthologies.

.

Marcus Cornaro
Ambassador of the European Union to South Africa

A note on translation

by Innocentia Mhlambi

The selected poems have been extrapolated from a larger submission to the Sol Plaatje European Union Literary Competition. However, while these poems made the selection, there are general translation issues that invariably affect all poems considered for entry into the competition. All poems aim for comprehension, thus simple isiZulu has been used in composing the poems and the translations have aimed to capture the simplicity of the language. Examples of this can be seen in 'Obaba abangebaba' or 'Ngenze Nami Ngiziqhenye'. There are instances where even the simplicity of the language does not guarantee comprehension by readers. This happens when a number of other language uses are deployed by the poets to affect greater poetics. For instance, all poems draw lavishly from oral art. This is a taxonomy of indigenous verbal plays with language forms which were in the past transposed verbatim by older generations to younger ones. These oral art forms include proverbs, sayings, idioms, folktales, riddles, songs, epithets, names, children's games and performance elements including rituals, dance and so forth. All poems considered made use of one or more of these forms and since, at times, there are no English equivalents for these culturally bound forms of expression, the translations aim for a loose approximation that ensure that meaning is not lost. Consider the poem, 'Icala Aliboli', and 'Ithemba Alibulali', the latter being made up only of proverbs strung together to form one major meaning which emphasises the existence of hope against all odds in life. In one poem, however, there was a reworking of

English idiomatic sayings into isiZulu, e.g. the appropriation of crocodile tears as 'izinyembezi zengwenya' in 'Obaba abangobaba'.

At times the poems make reference to popular songs, but then the reference is so slight that the meaning might be lost. One example is in 'Icala Aliboli'. There is a reference to a song, 'Amagugu alelizwe ayosala emathuneni', however, in the song only the phrase, 'sesingawaculela ngisho amagugu' appears. This is a hidden reference that entails that readers should know their popular songs very well. Still on this aspect, at times poems make reference to prominent social organisations that merge with the Christian social ordering of gender roles within the church, e.g. there is a reference to 'isililo somama besililo (Mothers' Union guilds) in 'Konakelephi', as well as references to the oral histories of the Zulu people and the outcry and outpouring of emotions occasioned by the death of Queen Nandi, the mother of King Shaka kaSenzangakhona.

In other instances the poems draw from biblical stories. In 'Konakelephi' there is a reference to post-1994 South Africa using the dialectics of Canaan and Egypt. 'Unisa' begins by reproducing what is believed to be what Jesus said about getting into heaven, that He is the only way. At times the references are to the turbulent 1980s black history of struggle, as in 'Ngiyadideka'. The repertoires of violence that dotted the past are brought to bear on the post-1994 situation when now a black government fails to do the will of the people. With all these references, when the context is not known by the readers, the meaning is lost.

There are also instances when the original words have

been retained because the references do not have readily available English worldviews, e.g. in the poem 'Ngenze Nami Ngiziqhenye', names of indigenous trees have been left unchanged: uMdoni, uMsinsi and uMsilinga. These names of trees point to deeper ontological features of the language which are also applicable elsewhere in the usage of the language, e.g. Muhle njengondoni yamanzi (as beautiful as a water lily) or uNjengomdoni (the tree that is found where water lilies will be found), or unguMsinsi wokuzimilela (s/he is a native). Thus these names were left unchanged for they point to deeper cosmological and epistemological aspects that open up the oral world which otherwise would be closed off if the English equivalents were sought.

One poem opens with a divination ritual, 'uNozigidi', where the diviner's chants are retained: 'Nginezigidi bhula Mangothobane' (I have millions divine you diviner of Mangothoban), using an archaic form of translation once dominant in the translation of praise poetry. Interestingly, the poem moves on to deal with complex issues related to liquor, lubricated cultures and hyper-consumerism where individuals given to hedonistic lifestyles are also subject to criminal targeting, thus moving away from the traditional premises with which it opens the poem. Readers must pay attention to this internal movement.

The poem mentioned above is 'Ngiyaphicaphica'. It includes a riddle; however, the answer to this riddle is not in the poem but in what readers find from working out the cues. Thus it entails a higher cognitive activity, which is outside the realm of the poem but somewhere in the reader's knowledge and understanding of their existentialities.

ISIXHOSA

Ndisithand'isiXhos'andiziva.
Ndisithand'isiXhos'andizenzi.
Kuthi ncooo! Kwikhuhlangubo, inkalakahla nencakra-
    ncakra yam xa kanti simahlath'aphuthinye.
Umlomo wam uba yingangalala, ungangomhlaba ukuba
    mkhulu kuku twebeka ngenxa yoncumo.
Amazinyo ibe ngath'ajing'emaweni kukungavaleki kwawo.
Ndiye ndibobotheke, amadol'adyevezele okunga
    ndiphimiswa ngumfana xa iintombi noonyana
    bakaPhalo besithetha.
Yiva ezizandi xa bethetha "Ndixabene nogxa wam ngenxa
    ye xoxo. Siye sabamba ingxoxo, saluxazulula olu
    xanduva, saze saxolelana."
"Yena utata kaQondile akaqondanga waze waqubul'igqudu
    wandibeth'enkqayi."

IsiXhosa lulwimi olumnandi.
IsiXhosa sikwenz'usebenzis'amathamb'enqondo.
Awukwazi usuke usebenzise igama nje kungekho sivakalisi.
Mamela, Ithanga – eli silityayo (umfuno), eli lisentla
    komlenze, nesinxibo sangaphantsi esinxitywa
    ngabasetyhini.
UmXhosa othetha isixhos'uliciko, kuba unezangotshe.
Zangotshe ezo zibhentsis'ubukrelekrele benqondo.
Mv'ezithutha – Thahla, Ndayeni, Ziqelekazi,
    Ngqungqushe, Hlamba ngobubend'amanz'ekhona,
    Nyawuza, Mpondo, Dakhile.
Umve omnye esithi-Mbathane, Xesibe, Nondzaba, Mnune
    mkhuma, Matshaya.

UmXhos'uzingqin'azidle ngobuXhosa bakhe-ngesiXhosa
esisulungekileyo esebenzis'izaci namaqhalo.
UmXhos'uzingqin'azidle ngobuXhosa bakhe –
ngomngqungqo.
UmXhos'uzingqin'azidle ngobuXhosa bakhe – ngesinxibo
sakwaNtu.
UmXhos'uzingqin'azidle ngobuXhosa bakhe – ngamasiko
nezithethe.
Woowu! Mbone ngezo zimbo, edlisela.

Jonga, nangoku andikwazi ukubeka usiba phantsi.
Ndibhal'umlembelele kub'inqond'izinzile.
Awu madoda! Ndingamathe nolwimi nolulwimi.
Ndixolel'ukubhubha nalo mhla lwabhangiswa.

Yhini na mawethu!
Yhini na mzontsundu!
Khuselani olulwimi nibe sisikhukukazi
sikhusel'amantshontsh'aso kukhetshe.
Mzali fundis'umntwan'ulwimi lweenkobe.
Mlisela nomthinjana mus'ukutyhila ngesidanga
soluny'uhlanga.
Ewe! Singangakwazi ukusibhala, kuba kaloku sifundiswe
ngabasentshona.
Mandulo ibi ngumnqa kuthi lo.
Kodwa noko – Yhini ukungasithethi.
Masingade sifundiswe ngabo noko.

IsiXhosa siyamakh'umntu!
IsiXhosa siliyeza kum!

ZUKISWA MURIEL ADONIS

THE XHOSA LANGUAGE

I like Xhosa language too much!
I don't know what to do without it.
If we are on the same page I am glad,
Joyful is my epiglottis, tongue and my other parts.
My mouth is widened as I smile broadly.
As if my teeth are hanging from a cliff.

I smile while my knees shake when one proposes love,
Especially when Phalo's sons speak isiXhosa.
Just listen to these sounds as they speak:
"I am at loggerheads with my friend because of a frog.
We discussed, solved the problem
And have forgiven each other."

"Qondile's father did not understand,
He took a knobkerrie and beat my bald head."
IsiXhosa is a nice language.
It causes you to think fast.
Words are used in sentences.
Listen, ithanga – it means pumpkin (as in the vegetable).
It also refers to the upper thigh.
The part women cover with tights.

An eloquent Xhosa speaker uses figurative speech,
That shows the speaker's wisdom. Listen to his Clan names!
Thatha, Ndayeni, Ziqelekazi, Ngqungqushe, Hlamba
    ngobubende!
Whereas there is water.
Nyawuza, Mpondo, Dakhile!
Another one says: "Mbathane, Xesibe, Nondzaba, Mnune,

Mkhuma, Matshaya!"

This man is proud of his isiXhosa, his pure first language.
He uses proverbs, phrases and figurative speech.
He is proud of his traditional dance, his traditional attire!
He is proud of his traditions and customs.
Observe him when he is busy with traditional dance!

Even now I can't put down my pen!
I write continuously because my mind is stable.
Look guys, I am taken up by this language!
I am prepared to die when that language is banned!

My countrymen, homeboys! Protect this language like a hen!
Which protects its chickens from eagles.
Parent! Teach your child your home language!
Teenagers, don't be taken up by other languages!
Yes, we may be unable to write isiXhosa if we were taught by white people.
Long ago we could not believe that.

Yet we are bound to speak isiXhosa!
We must not allow Western people to teach us isiXhosa.
IsiXhosa builds a human being.
IsiXhosa is like medicine to me!

Translated from the Xhosa original – Zukiswa Muriel Adonis's IsiXhosa – by Angelinah Dazela

THE ATTACK OF THE PESTS

English

My father never taught me
how to catch rats.

I'm lucky to be growing up
with neither famine nor war,
he said. But I'm persistent, always asking questions.

"What's it like to eat rat?"
"If cooked just right, they taste almost like chicken."
"What about the fur? The snout?
The tail? The little paws and feet, those fingers?"

Father's stare cut right through me
as if in search of something running
and hiding among the foliage.

The veins on his neck grew
visible, the bones in his hands
leapt with the momentary jerk.

All of a sudden I felt cold,
swept away by his stare: a world
I wish not to see.

JIM PASCUAL AGUSTIN

HONDEDROLLE OP DIE GRASPERK
Afrikaans

Allie huise waar ons verby ry se grasse
Is gloeiend groen
Soos ry tekens
En blare bloeiend

ma vra of die woord regtig "begraafplaas" is
sonder om 'n antwoord te wil anker
anders luister ek
na die woord asof haar tong dit reeds veras het

allie huise waar ons verby ry se grasse
is grafte
waarin broer se drug addiction
waarin pa se swye
waarin ma se ineenstortings
R.I.P.

met hondedrolle soos ruikers daarop geplant.

                              DU TOIT ALBERTZE

DOG SHIT ON THE LAWN

The lawns of all the houses we drive past
are glowingly green
like go signs
and bleeding leaves

Mom asks if it's really called "burial ground"
without trying to anchor an answer
otherwise I listen
to the words like her tongue has already cremated them

The lawns of all the houses we drive past
are graves
where brother's drug addiction
dad's silence
mom's breakdowns
R.I.P.

with dog shit planted like flowers on top

Translated from the Afrikaans original – Du Toit Albertze's Honde Drolle op die Grasperk – by Pieter Odendaal

BRAAI

Afrikaans

Aan allie tannies da' diep innie Namakwaland
Wa' die kokerbome die mense ophys
Ennie mense die blomme se koppe afkap
Da wa' julle my moffiewees wou wegwaai
Met julle bidgroepies
Hande ommie braai

Hierrie vuur brand vir julle

Want moffies moker al op hul mooiste
Met kliphakke
En leeuvel-tiertertjies
Lank voor Christus sy patriargale pote kom pons het op
 ons planeet

Ons is profete
Soos Jonathan wat sy kleed laat val het
En voor Dawid gekniel het
Vir jou min ek meer as weelde en vroue en konginkryk
En hul kraak inmekaar
Mense vergeet sommige verse inni bybel
Lees sommer net Levitikus en Romeine raak
Jy kani sekere goed uit-edit of crop of forward nie
Glo my
Ons weet
Want moffies moker al op hul mooiste
Met kliphakke
En leeuvel-tiertertjies
Lank voor Christus sy patriargale pote kom pons het op
 ons planeet

Ons is soldate
Soosie manne oppie grens wat genaai het tussen landmyne
    en agter sandduine
Maar net sekeres is aangehou in hospitale
Geskok
Pille gevoer
Manwees afgeslag
Want mense weet tot vandag toe nie die verskil tussen
'n vrou wat 'n vrou wil wees
En 'n man wat 'n man wil hê nie

Moffies moker al op hul mooiste
Met kliphakke
En leeuvel-tiertertjies
Lank voor Christus sy patriargale pote kom pons het op
    ons planeet

Ek ween want Ma wil hê ek moet 'n nageslag verweef
En miljoene vrou word gekorrigeer, opgevoed, gedwing
Om mans te aanbid
Dood gestenig in Paarl
Deur familie
Gesodomiseer in Strand
En hulle noem ons die barbare
Al gons hul van primitiwiteit

Maar wat hulle nie weet nie
Is dat ons al lankal hierso is
Met Griekse orgies en Spartan tente vol daddies en twinks

Liewe tannies van Namakwaland
Waar die kokerbome die mense ophys
Ennie mense die blomme afkap
As ek die brandwonde op my arms moes tel
Dan sal dit steeds nie die skade kon bewys
Maar julle kon dalk hande vat om 'n vuur
Maar julle sal nooit ons vuur blus
Wat woester brand as Knysna

Manne laat wegkyk sodat hul oë nie brand nie

Ons was al lankal hier
So, pasop
Die moffies is op pad
Een veldbrand
Op
'n
Slag

                DU TOIT ALBERTZE

BRAAI

To all the tannies in the heart of Namaqualand
Where quiver trees hoist people up
And people cut down flower heads
There where you tried to blow away my queerness
With your prayer groups
Hands around the braai

This fire burns for you

Because moffies have been beautifully striking back
With stone heels
And lionskin tiger tartlets
Long before Christ pounced his paws on our planet

We are prophets
Like Jonathan who dropped his cloak
To kneel before David
I love you more than wealth and women and kingdom
And they creak into each other
People forget certain bible verses
Only read Leviticus and Romans
You can't edit-out or crop or forward certain things
Believe me
We know
Because moffies have been beautifully striking back
With stone-heels
And lionskin tiger tartlets
Long before Christ pounced his paws on our planet

We are soldiers
Like the men on the border who fucked between
    landmines and behind sand dunes
But only some were held in hospitals
Shocked
Fed pills
Manhood flayed
Because people still don't know the difference between
A woman who wants to be a woman
And a man who wants a man

Moffies have been beautifully striking back
With stone heels
And lionskin tiger tartlets
Long before Christ pounced his paws on our planet

I cry because Ma wants me to weave a progeny
And millions of women are corrected, educated, forced
To worship men
Stoned to death in Paarl
By family
Sodomised in Strand
And they call us barbaric
While they're abuzz with primitiveness

But what they don't know
Is that we've been here for a long time
With Greek orgies and Spartan tents full of daddies and
    twinks

Dear tannies from Namaqualand
Where quiver trees hoist people up
and people cut down flowers
If I had to count the burn wounds on my arms
They would still not prove the damage
Though you can hold hands around a fire
You will never extinguish ours
Burning fiercer than Knysna

Making men look away so their eyes don't burn

We've been here for a long time
So watch out
The moffies are coming
One veldfire
At
A
Time

Translated from the Afrikaans original – Du Toit Albertze's Braai – by Pieter Odendaal

THERE IS

English

There is a white man that is whiter than a bridge of bone
Across to the stars or the township. There is a shaking
Hand that is firmer than burned iron in a falling missile.

There is a grimace underneath your skull every Passover,
And Christmas too. There is a drowned voyage home
That rises up and down your legs like a tide every night.

There is a place of stone where you lie like a grave and
    earth passes under.

There is a dead body in your room that you must carry
Outside into the garden, a winter wind hot with fallen
    leaves
And the coming fire. A heaviness in your bones made
Of you and all your sense of failure heavy like a broken
    down car.
A hot breath on the window separating us from nothing.
A bleeding hand that puts back together your silent mirror
    on the wall.
A snake that sleeps and waits for summer to come.

                                            KYLE ALLAN

JUST THE LYNTJIE

BILINGUAL

She doesn't have a gold tooth entirely.
Just a gold line on the tip of the tooth.
On the left.
Just the lyntjie.
Subtle.

The brown gentry are buying lentils
She's still working the tills

She can't go to school cause she's moeggenaai
Sarag is it nog dop en braai
Naar from her Rothmans Blue
She's tired of looking at you

Swaarkry willie versakkie
Genuine nie majatie
Vedala ma nie verleppie
Gham ma noggie smettie
Hand issie 'n tettie
Gat gan sy nie lekkie

MIA ARDERNE

NSATI WA MAKARATA

XITSONGA

Eka Lutendo wa le Block C, Mpheni

Ndzi ri njanganja leyo thya makarata a yi ndzi suki,
I huma hi 6 nimixo a vuya na vusiku, hoo!
Swihlangi swo ti layitela; swo tivondzela.
U thamuka-thamuka le makaratini na xidonchi xo twa mati
[5]Onge o rindzela masiku; ku vona n'weti!

Mina hwititi, mali ndza rhumela, hayi swingwece n'wana mhani,
Kambe yo hundzuka mali ya vhuza.
Xixevo a nga xavi; girosa ya kona i atcher, matandza na ticondzo
Vananga va dya rikoko ra xilondza.
[10]Society ya kolota; mali ya minkosi egangeni ndza kolota.

Swibvanani swa ganga leri swi na mikhuva ya thyaka,
Ku thyiwa makarata peta-peta,
Ku lumekiwa makhandhlela swi ta nyanga kahle,
Onge hi le mirindzelweni wa Mbhazima,
[15]Mahuza lawa, ma fanela hi mahlo ya swimanga.

Nsati wa makarata ndzi phula ti hola!
Loko a tiva ku na vuya hi Ravunthlanu, month-end,
U ta fona: "Vha khou swika ngafhi muthu wanga?
  Baba, yo kuloka na tshelede?"
[20]Ivi mina ndzi n'wayitela hi ku xurha mifututu ya nghomondhela

Swandla swakwe swi fehlelela no nyakalela makarata –
Ku nga ri ku vukarha makatla yanga, a ndzi kandza no ndzi thova.
A nga lavi ku ndzi swoswa-swoswa khwatsi; ndzi vuyelela eka xikhale xanga,
Kumbe ku ndzi ntswotswa-ntswotswa xitswatsi ndzi nga gayisa-ka;
25Yena i gogosani; u gogosela ntsanda wa gwama ra le mugodini le Burgersfort.

Loko ndzi ku gaa, "Khotsi a Mpho, kha vha litshe vhuname, vha bvise gwama…"
Hi leswiyaa, hudya-hudya, u ya tlanga makarata na swibvanani swa muganga
"Bavoo, mi nga vileli
Le makaratini a ku na xivundza
30Nakona ndzi nga va na nkateko ndzi wina siku rin'wana…"

A nga ndzi swekeli. A nga ndzi hlantsweli.
N'wi byeli hi minkumba, heyi, onge o va na nyawa!
Leswo ndzi hosi yo kha miroho Mpheni-jikelele ya tiva;
Na yena wa tivuyisa, u cina onge o hlola.
35Hi xinyanyu, na le kerekeni a nga byi vika vumbhoni lebyi!

Kambe mali ya mina nyikiri yi helela emakarateni –
Yi vundza emindzhutini ya makhandhlela na swidonci.
Jarata i machokolobyanyi; kaya ra nhlarhu ni swimbi swa yona.

I xikhwatana; ku lo hudya hi mahlwehlwe, mixiji a
   magwanda.
⁴⁰Exitangeni onge i nkombiso, nkhuvu wa mahele-
swihahampfhuka.

Kamara ya hina i bakwa minkokolombani na swipululu.
Malerhi ya n'wana hi mpfhuka ya lovekiwa hi lembe ra
   timbyana.
Tlhu-tlhu-tlhuuu! Tlhu-tlhu-tlhuuu!
Poto ra mukhotyo-xiseluselu bya, byaa, byaaa!
⁴⁵Loyi wansati i n'anga ya vufendze man'!

Ticece ta hina i timbyana ta rikwekwe,
Ti lo pyii, ti ku vikuu, hi thyaka:
Rhwembu-rhwembu, rhwembu-rhwembu!
Ximutani xa kona ku beriwa mati endzhaku ka guda,
⁵⁰Ko nguu, onge hi le xipotweni.

Vana va birimile onge papa a nga thevukeli.
Onge ndzi ndhoza, ndzi bolele hi mbewu.
Macakala ya vananga i minkuxi; mepe wa Afrika na
   swihlala!
Swiburukwani i timboni ta golonyi hala ndzhaku,
⁵⁵Swi boxeke na matsolo ku nga ri fexeni ya
van'waswinyeketi.

Zodwa, nsati wa madyondza, u hume hi bya muphye hi
   vunjanganja –
Lexiya a ku ri jajangu marherhwani number one!
Xibazana xa mani na mani,

Xifaki va khumuzelanaku,
⁶⁰Na yena a ambala khancu a gandzela makarata.

Loko ti pyile; a lo khekhexwa –
Leya matlhari yi tlanga hi yena;
Yi n'wi xavela swigaywana na xinyamani –
Hakelo wa yi tiva; leswi xisuti xi nga fihla bakwa ra
   vulombe ke? Na xifuva xi nga yima-ke?
⁶⁵Va ta hakula swihlenge na mabvana!

"Wansati, u hluphekela yini
U manyele xipaci exikarhi ka milenge ya wena…?
U byambula njhani, dada ra musangu u hiwile…?
Va tshiki va chaya xingomani xexo,
⁷⁰Tundunduu, tundunduu!

Wena olela tirhandi na ya maphepha u lo hwi!
Hluva, juvela minkuku yaleyo u rhunge nomo!
Hi siku ra makumu u nga vutisiwa:
Xana u endlile yini hi nhundzu leyi ndzi ku nyikeke?
⁷⁵Swa antswa i ku: Va tlhuvutsile le makaratini bavoo!"

Bayizani na yena u le ndleleni,
U ta gotsa maguja a huma hi bya muphye,
U ta huma a ri tani, a ri cheleni!
Ndzi karhele hi swiyutha swa makarata,
⁸⁰Onge swi lo dyisiwa ricondo ra mhangele.

Lava mina ndzi va kumaka, a hi vatshiveri –
I vatimi va ndzilo hi mati na misava.

Mhani a va tipfinyingi:
N'wananga a wu na voko,
[85]Tiyimayimi; u nga etleli na mabutsu.

Na hahani i khale va swi vona:
Famba u ya lavisisa; kumbe u ya hlahluvela,
U ta wisa van'wahuveni, u wisa magelegele.
Loko swi nga ri tano; xitiko xi ta ku nthii!
[90]Muti wa Mudau ku sala marhumbi.

                    VONANI BILA

A WIFE THAT PLAYS CARDS

Dear Lutendo from block C, Mpheni.

A woman who pays cards does not fascinate me.
She goes out at 6am and comes back late at night.
Children are forced to light up and make means to cook for themselves,
She pops in and out where she plays her cards.
⁵She always anticipates the end of the month as if she has been waiting for more than the set number of days of the month!

I always send her good money, not cents my brother.
But to her it is just money spent on unnecessary things
She does not buy meat; her type of groceries is atchar, eggs and chicken feet. My kids eat leftovers.
She owes the stockvel;
¹⁰The kids in our community are naughty and have bad habits.

They play cards from sunrise to sunset,
They even light up candles so that they can have better sight and continue to play.
They do this as if it was Mbhazima's night vigil.
¹⁵The drawings on their faces (unordered women) would look good on the eyes of a cat.

A woman who plays cards! I despise.
When she knows that I am coming back Friday, month-end,
She will call me: "what time will you be here my person?"

Father is the money delayed as well?
[20]Then I consider that maybe am tired of all this.

Her hands are the ones that shuffle and hand out cards.
She should not wish for me to make things right; and
   return to my rigid ways.
Or maybe find myself someone else.
[25]She does nothing all day long at Burgersfort.

When I look at her she utters "Mpho's father, please stop
   being stingy and give me some money."
There they go, off to play cards with children from the
   community.
Father do not doubt anything.
When playing cards, there is no boredom.
[30]One day luck will be on my side and I will win.

She does not cook nor wash for me.
If you tell her about the blankets, she becomes sick
   instantly.
The entire Mpheni knows that I am a kind chief that
   harvests his own greens.
She dances in a forbidden manner.
[35]At church she does nothing.

But my money she spends on cards.
She lives in the shadow of a candle, just for the sake of
   playing cards.
The yard is a mess.
[40]If you went inside the house, you would think that

cockroaches are having an exhibition.

Our room is the same as a cave filled with crawling insects.
Used dippers have been left exposed for a while now.
In the kitchen there is a boiling pot
The lid of the pot falls off.
[45]This woman has a doctorate in being untidy!

The dirt of our items equals the dirt of a dog
They are very dirty.
In the toilet people pee on the wall.
[50]In that house, people pee just behind the walls as if it was in a tavern.

The kids look like they have no father figure.
As if my seed died.
My kids' clothes are dirty and in parts like the map of Africa
Their trousers have holes,
[55]They are torn up on the knee areas, you cannot claim its fashion.

Zodwa, the first wife, lost out on her marriage because of such foolishness.
She was the first love
Every man did as they would wish with her.
She is like corn, men share her.
[60]She wore a jacket and shoved into the jacket her cards.

When she gets drunk,
men take her for a fool;
they win her over by buying her maize.
You know the result of such things; what will happen now
 that you are pregnant?
^{65}And your breasts are heavily out!

"Woman, what do you suffer from?
You put your wallet in your legs?
How do you do it?
let them play their own song.
^{70}Tundunduu, tundunduu!

Just collect all the money in silence!
Do everything in silence.
on the last day, do not ask any questions
What did you do with the items (money/clothes) I gave
 you?!"
^{75}It's better that I say;

Bayizani (another) is also on the way.
You will pack your things and leave like a nobody,
You shall leave with nothing on your body, and nothing to
 your name!
I am tired of this life of you playing cards
^{80}As if someone placed a spell on you.

Those I find, don't conform!
They stop bad things with everything they have.
A mother does not treat herself bad.

My child you do not have a hand,
[85]Don't sleep with you boots on.

Even your aunt has seen this for a while now:
go and enquire, or go see a traditional healer,
You will take a break from all these noise makers.
If it does not happen that way, you will be left all alone!
[90]The only thing to remain in this house will be Mudau's bones.

Translated from the Xitsonga original – Vonani Bila's Nsati Wa Makarata – by Aubrey Neo Sehlahla

BONTEHEUWEL

Afrikaans

Wat maak ek hier met my hart
in my hande en my rug
teen die muur

die tikpyp omgestuur,
gloeilamp, klein kalbas
tuisgeblaas uit afvalglas

'n Halfmaan mans
dryf op wolke en 'n vlam,
die rook bol wit
soos die seile van 'n skip

onderweg na Waar de goede hoop

'n Labirint van redding en verraad
middelherfs weer uitgespeel
in die sinkhok waar ons sit
by daggapitte en strooitjies

Ons gedeelde voorsate flikker
in die slawelosie van kristal

Vlugtelinge en bannelinge
verewig in sand om die voete
van 'n kind in doeke,
offerlam van die Vlakte

    RENÉ BOHNEN

BONTEHEUWEL

Why am I here with my heart
in my hands and my back
against the wall

the tik pipe is passed around,
a light bulb, tiny calabash
of home-blown scrap glass

A crescent moon of men
floats on clouds and a flame,
the smoke billowing white
as the sails of a ship

en route to the Where of good hope

A maze of grace and deceit
replayed this mid-autumn
in the shack where we sit
amid straws and ganja pips

Our shared ancestors glimmer
in the crystal slave lodge

Exiles and refugees
immortalised in sand around the feet
of a child in nappies,
sacrificial lamb of the Flats

*Translated from the Afrikaans original – René Bohnen's
Bonteheuwel – by René Bohnen*

THE THIRST

ENGLISH

In my dream
I watch the rain fall
through me,
no puddles form at my feet.

Only the sun
washes the earth,
stones crumble,
clouds are swallows flying north.

I am a beggar
on my knees,
the moon a
communion wafer.

      CHRISTINE COATES

IKAGENG

ENGLISH

There are doves here in Ikageng,
the house at the far end,
over the bridge, under the slipway,
up through the industrial area.
Ikageng's small dusty yards,
the street signs are broken and I'm lost.
Past voices shriek,
then a fruit vendor comes to help.

Martha gives me her colonial name
but I know it's Mojabeng. She says
"This is your home."
In her brick house my room is shiny,
everything covered in plastic.
Her room is in the yard.
A man from Eskom, the other guest.
The doves here line up on the wall waiting.

When my car won't start, Eskom helps me.
What will I do if it won't start in the dark?
"Someone will help you," he says.
There are doves here in Ikageng.
At midnight I lie listening to them cooing
in the rafters, and the township music,
people softly talking, watching TV.
Slowly the sounds die down, a dog barks.

A muezzin wakes me. It's 5.37 am.
the morning cars rev engines in the cold,
a band strikes up a practice.

I make tea and slowly unfold into the township day.
At a table outside I write and watch children off to school,
smiling, playing, they peer in over the gate and greet me.
And the doves – there are doves here
in Ikageng.

CHRISTINE COATES

ULWANDLE

ISIXHOSA

Ndithe ndisabethwa yimpepho yolwandle
Ndisathi ukuva intsholo yamaza elwatyuza
Qhaphu gqi ndoda ithile
Imnyama thsu ngokwebala
Yahlala ecaleni kwam ngakwisandla sasekhohlo
Indithe ndunya ngamehlo angenamnqandi
Ndizamile ukumqala ngelenkobe
Wandithi ntsho emehlweni ephefumlela phezulu
Zaxanananza ingcinga, ndangcangcazela zangcazelana
  imbambo
Ndaqonda mandicaphule kwelasemzini ndathi "hi"
Akenza nesandi uthe bhaxa esitulweni
Ndaqhaqhazela ndagodola ngesiquphe
Wanditshutshisa umchamo

Eloxesha ndinoncumo olungcangcazelayo
Kuthe ngeli-ngeni
Walatha ezindlebeni umfana wakuthi wanikina
Ndimthe ntsho ngalommehlo agcwele impixano
Udwanduluke wathi "I am no speaking English person, I
  am a Kenyan."
Kwexibilili. Ndaphakamisa oobhontsi ndanqwala intloko
Uphinde walatha ebusweni bam wamncuma, waphakamisa
  oobhontsi
Ndancuma oloncumo luyekeyeke
Waphakama wahamba
Ingcinga yintilongo nenkululeko yobom.

SILULUNDI COKI

THE SEA

I was enjoying the sea breeze.
Listening to the galloping waves.
A pitch-black man appeared.
He sat close, on my left-hand side.
He stared at me without blinking his eyes.

I tried to speak to him,
Using my African language.
He was breathing fast, I thought deeply.
My ribs were shaking as I tried to say, "Hi".
Glued on his chair he said nothing.

I forced a smile as I wanted to urinate.
Later the guy touched his ears and shook his head.
Being confused I stared at him while he said,
"I am no English speaking person, I am a Kenyan."

Lifting my thumbs, I nodded as my fears were gone.
Looking at me he smiled and lifted his thumbs.
I forced a smile as he stood and left me.
Thinking of prison and freedom of life.

*Translated from the Xhosa original – Silulundi Coki's Ulwandle –
by Angelinah Dazela*

KANTI NIYAHLUPHA!

IsiXhosa

Mizwa ndini uqhekez'ubuchopho
Uxaba uxam adideke de adadazele
Uyinto apha etlubula ubumi bobomi
Powu! Uyahlupha nto ndini.

Uthi wakundintantathekise ndizive ndililolo ebantwini.
Ingaba uyinto esukaphi kusini na?
Imini nobusuku uyandinxaphisa.
Mihla nezolo ndididekile
Ngcambu zini ezi zakumilosayo, unyulu.
Powu! Uyahlupha nto ndini

Tyhini kuzizijwili ekuhlaleni ngenxa yakho
Kaloku thina bantu bantsundu adibazi ubungangamsha
    bakho
Ndibeka iziphoso kwabamandulo
Ndililela abazali ngokungakukhankanyi
Tyhini mizwa kanti nawe uyingxenya yobomi?
Powu! Uyahlupha nto ndini

Jonga ngoku mizwa ndini uthatha isigqibo ngobomi bam
    ndirhole amehlo
Kanti ukuze ndichulumance ingaba funeka ndenze ntoni
    na?
Yazi xa ubulumko bufana nobudenge kuthethwa le nto
Ndibopha ndiyeka, imbandezelo ziyathontelana
Unyulu, wenza izinto ezimanyukunyezi
Uyahlupha nto ndini

SILULUNDI COKI

YOU BRING DISCOMFORT

You feelings, you crack my skull.
You even make someone unstable.
You strip someone of his life.
No! You are a troublesome thing!

I become lonely when you ruin me.
Where do you come from by the way?
Day and night you make me restless!
I get confused on a daily basis!
Which roots have anchored you?
Are you pure? No! You are troublesome!

You brought unhappiness to the society.
We, black people, do not know your strength.
I always blame my ancestors,
Our parents never mentioned you!
Oh, conscience is also part of our lives!
No! You are a troublesome thing!

Look, you make decisions about my life!
That happens right under my nose.
What must I do to be happy?
I thought I was wise, while I am being foolish!
I am helpless while problems are piling.
Conscience, you are pure, but you frustrate us!
No! You are a troublesome thing!

Translated from the Xhosa original – Silulundi Coki's Kanti Niyahlupha! – by Angelinah Dazela

IINWELE

IsiXhosa

Yintsika nobuhle kwabaninzi
De bacaphule kwezase Ntshona
Ibenza bazingce baqhashazele
Banyoshoze bajije izinqa
De bachul'ukunyathela

Tyhini! yintsika nobuhle kwabaninzi
Kodwa zikho izangxa ezibetha ngempenyelele nevithala
Ezithi xa zihlohla ikama kukhale amanqanqanqa
Ezithi zakuthi phethuthu ngezontlokwana zazo zicinge ngcono

Tyhini! Kukhala ibhungane kweminye imizi ngenxa yezinwele zodidi
Kwabasetyhini le yingxoxo yemihla nezolo
Xa iyintoni ebangela ucaphule unwele?
Ingaba kungazazi na nto zakuthi?
Uyakukuxhwithwa ngezonzipho zikanomgrwabayi
ngamanenekazi wakukukhankanya oko

Tyhini! Le nto ilinwele inzulu kanti?
Xa kutheni le nto sinenwele ezahlukileyo nje?
Nto yakuthi zinikithuba ucinge inwele zomAfrika omhle.
Ziqothololo, zigqagqene uyakufika enye ithe qelele kwenye
Zizoba ubume be Afrika iphela

Ziqulathe intsingiselo enzulu ngemvelaphi yethu.
MaAfrika amahle khanakheni imikhanya nityebise amehlo

Tyhini! Iyanconywa into xa intle
Zingce ngento onayo mAfrika wakowethu
Yintsika nobuhle kwabaninzi

SILULUNDI COKI

THE HAIR

It is a pillar and beauty to many people,
They even mix it with hair from the West.
Hair fills people with pride and confidence.
They walk tall and swing their waists.
As they move they mind their steps.

Of course, hair is attraction to many people.
But too thick hair needs attention.
As you comb it there's noise and groaning.
Combed hair makes people think properly.
Other homes are empty because of quality hair.

Females debate about hair on a daily basis.
What causes you to add strange hair to yours?
Is it because we do not know ourselves?
With sharp nails one will pinch your hair.
Ladies don't want you to mention the pinching.

Oh! Hair goes deeply into your skull!
Why is our hair different?
Just think about an African's hair!
It consists of scattered hard pieces.
Our hair resembles the shape of Africa.

Our hair is about our origin.
Fellow Africans, please be observant!

Give credit if something is beautiful.
Fellow African, be proud of what you have!
It is a pillar and beauty to many of us!

Translated from the Xhosa original – Silulundi Coki's Inwele – by Angelinah Dazela

MONT AUX SOURCES – THE LIGHTNING

ENGLISH

Your thunderous applause
echoes through the valleys
of my mind, plucking my strings
from primordial past, to present tense

        MARK DE WET

DELAYED OBITUARY

ENGLISH

faith here is not the obliteration
of the air between two palms,
words limping out of a torn mouth,
rising to come down
as what we will to be rain.
no, it is not. it is something close
to the small miracle of this woman
biding time, washing clothes,
    hanging them on a washing line
to claim all heat of a tomorrow
that cannot find home in her hand.

    LUTHANDO DLAMINI

(AUSCHWITZ)-BIRKENAU 2 SHOE
English

That shoe –
Singled,
Out,
Amongst a multitude of horrors.

That red shoe –
Set aside
From the muddled tower of

    black
    brown
    broken
    booted

That red, embroidered shoe –
High-heeled,
Waiting:
For an elegant curve of foot,
The slide of silk stockings,
The golden tap on a wooden floor,
A glide of dance on a star-bright night.

That foot.
In darkness.
Arching away from cold cement.

Still.

               RUTH EVERSON

NAMHLANJE NDIVULELE IHAGU ESITIYENI SIKA TATA

IsiXhosa

Namhlanje ndivulele ihagu
Esitiyeni sika Tata
Ndayi bukela ivuthulula idlakaza izityalo
Ezatyalwa ngabazali bam ngothando

Namhlanje ndivulele ihagu
Esitiyeni sika Tata
Ndixakiwe nokuba ndiza kuphendula ndithini
Xa ndibuzwa ngemifuno neziqhamo

Namhlanje ndivulele ihagu
Esitiyeni sika Tata
Kuba indi qhathe ngobu newu-newu
Yandithembisa ngama nqatha ayo

Namhlanje ndivulele ihagu
Esitiyeni sika Tata
Kuba bendifuna ukufana nabanye
Ndidle ubuncwane bobomi

Namhlanje ndiya zisola
Ngoba ndivulele ihagu esitiya
Esitiyeni sika Tata!

NOBUNTU GANTANA

A PIG IN THE GARDEN

Today I let a pig in my father's garden.
I had been watching when it scattered the plants,
That were planted by my loving parents.

Today I let a pig in my father's garden.
I do not know how to respond,
When my parents ask about their fruit and vegetables.

Today I let a pig in my father's garden.
I was gullible when the pig promised me riches.
It promised its fat and I foolishly believed it.

Today I let a pig in my father's garden.
I wanted to be like the elite,
And enjoy luxury life while being in the limelight.

Today I let a pig in my father's garden.
But I really regret, I should not have allowed,
This pig to be in my father's garden!

Translated from the Xhosa original – Nobuntu Gantana's Namhlanje ndivulele ihagu esitiyeni sika Tata – by Angelinah Dazela

TRIGGER WARNING SERIES

ENGLISH

One

My pain lives in a nest in my chest
regenerating with weeds
every time i set her on fire

Two

Your pain visits me in my dream.
I sleep with your violations.

Trigger warning: Three

I dream of a tree
growing hands not leaves,
thousands, with 1 to 7 fingers, all
with perfect finger nails
each fingernail bitten to the quick,
bleeding

blood running down my trunk

I do not know who bites the fingernails
I have no mouth
only porous earth to kiss you
or   set my earthworms on you.

The hands were birthed to
write to make wind songs or fists
or stroke each other gentle.

Each of them was pierced by a grain of sand
that grew into a blister
grew into a bone,
now   none of them can move.

My hope is in the soil
fed by the blood
fortified by industrious earthworms.

I cannot look down.
I fear the soil is rotting too.

: four

I dream that if i die
the hands will fall off the tree. All At Once.

the sky will be filled with moths

all falls cushioned.

all wings a song

                    SARAH GODSELL

PLEIADES

ENGLISH

The First Wife: uMaya
    Seleme se setshehadi*
    came from the West
    just before the reign,
    her hair on fire,
    and a silver fork sewn into her skirt,
    and a pale swirl above her ankle
    that flashed as she walked on shells.

The Second Wife: uLekhatle
    Less beautiful than the rest,
    more like a sister,
    her skin was as blue as feathers
    and her tongue tasted mellow
    like *uthanga*.

The Third Wife: uThakete
    On the anniversary of his first marriage
    the Warrior took in uThakete
    who swept the kraal with a fly-switch
    and then sat down outside the larder.
    She never stood up again.

The Fourth Wife: uAlkhayone
    From the class of cowherds,
    her bride price was small
    but her body was fat

---

*   The name for the constellation of the Pleiades, in Sesotho, meaning 'she who sows'. In Greek mythology the names of the Pleiades are: Maia, Electra, Taygete, Alcyone, Celaeno, Sterope, and Merope.

and her children prospered
like the leaves of trees
out of the reach of giraffes.

The Fifth Wife: uTselayeno
One leg shorter than the other
she moves on footprints
that circle the house
like the branches of thorn trees.
The snakes dare not pass.

The Sixth Wife: uSthelophe
When she sang, the people forgot
their loved ones who had drowned.
She taught the starlings to sing,
she taught the clouds to cry.

The Seventh Wife: uMelope
Eternally pursued
by the man with the arrow
and the spear, her spirit will wane
with the passing moon,
but she'll never be trapped
behind a rock or in the place
where the water skin has dripped
a pattern of stars
into the dust.

                    RICHARD HIGGS

SAL NOOIT 'N WITMAN DATE NIE
Afrikaans

Ek sal nooit 'n witman date nie
'Cause hulle loep mos net soe verby
Mens en kyk jou kak an
Dis hoekom ve'kyk ek my altyd so an die athletes
Wat skielik nou oori grêns date
Is cute.
Hulle fotos op Instagram is cute
En die kinders se hare love ek
Ma ôs wat soe van die kant af kyk
Weet mos wat klap so.
Any case
Een marag voori drama dans
Sê ek toe vir my chommie
Wiet djy, die manne kyk ons nou soe kak an
But eendag as os os droeme berykit
Dan is ôs skielik goed genoeg
Nou net om die rede, en die ander apartheid kak wat my
 ouma my so van vertel
Is alles die redes hoekom ek nooit 'n witman sal date nie.

VERONIQUE JEPHTAS

WILL NEVER DATE A WHITE MAN

I will never date a white man
'Cause they just walk past
You and look at you
That's why I always feast my eyes on the athletes
That are suddenly dating across the line
It's cute
Their photos on Instagram are cute
And I love the girls' hair
But we who stand on the sidelines
Know what's going on
Any case
One afternoon before the drama dance
I told my chommie
You know, they are looking at us like we're shit
But one day when we've reached our dreams
Then we'll suddenly be good enough
Now precisely because of this, and all the other apartheid
    shit that my grandma tells me about
Are all the reasons why I will never date a white man

Translated from the Afrikaans original – Veronique Jephtas's Sal Nooit 'n Witman Date Nie – by Pieter Odendaal

NGENZE NAMI NGIZIGQAJE

IsiZulu

Njalo uma ngibuka, ngiqalaza ngike ngicabange
Ngabe iMdoni, iMsinsi kanye neMsilinga
Kuzibuzani, kuzitshelani phambi kokumila
Uma isikhathi sonyaka sesikhulumile kuba njani?
Kungani mina ngivuma ukuzinyeza futhi ngizahlulela?
Angivume nami ngiqhakaze ngentokozo nangokuziqhenya.
Likhona na icala uma kunguwe s'thandwa sami
Ongenza ithemba kimi libuye?
Uma kunguwe ongangenza intombi ethandiweyo
    ngokuphelele,
kungabe ngicela lukhulu uma ngifisa ukwazi
lowo muzwa wothando olungenamkhawuko?
Ngivumele ngibe ngokhethekile ngibonwe nawusana.
Ngethembe ang'soze ngacela lutho olunye.

Haya ngami izinkondlo, uqambe ngami izingoma,
phupha ngami uphinde uvuke ngami.
Themba lami nami nginamaphupho, vuma siwafeze.
Emaphusheni nami ngi'bona ukubamba kwembungulu.
Ngisayokhalelani uma ngiqhakaze emehlweni akho
kuhle kwezimbali zomgxamo zona ezenza konke kube
    kuhle.
Ngenze nami ngikhohlwe usizi nabo bonke ububi
ngalo nje uthando lwakho oludlula olwabanye
lona oluthi lubanzi kanti lujulile,
olumtoti ngaphezu kwazo zonke iziphethu.
Ewu! Ngilomele ngaphezu kwakho konke,
impela ngizibona lungifanele!

Nanini nanini ngiyolukhumbula futhi ngiluthakasele

lona uthando lwakho engingakaze ngaluzwa emhlabeni.
Umama wami wasithela ngale kwezintaba, ubaba
　　ongizalayo yena waphangalala,
Ithemba lami selisele kuwe ngakho angifuni golide noma
　　isiliva
Kepha uma ukhona ngiyobe ngiphelele, nami ngiyoba
　　negama.
Mhla ngakubona, ngakwazi futhi ngakholwa uthando
　　lwakho
s'thandwa sami elethu liyakuba elingafelwa nkonyane.
Osekusele ukuba sihlangane, eyakho indawo kudala
　　ngayilungisa
Uthando olukimi lugcwele luyaphuphuma lulinde
　　lolosuku,
lapho uyovula emasangweni enhliziyo yami.
Izipho oyakube uziphethe ngiyozifica kweyakho inhliziyo
Yeka intokozo nemigubho esilindile!!

　　　　　　　　　　　　　　ZANDILE KHUMALO

MAKE ME PROUD OF MYSELF

When I look around sometime I wonder
Whether the Mdoni, the Msinsi and the Msilinga trees
Ever ask themselves before shooting?
When the time of the year has spoken, how things are?
Why do I consent to undermine myself and judge myself?
I must also agree to blossom with joy and be proud of
 myself.
Is there a crime if it is you my love
Who make hope to me return?
If it is you who make me a completely loved maiden
am I asking too much when I wish to feel
those unbounded emotions of love?
Allow me to be the chosen one so that even a baby can
 witness that
With hope I will never ask of anything else.

Recite poetry about me and compose songs about me
Dream of me and also when you awake think of me
My hope I also have dreams, consent that we bring them
 to fruition
In my dreams I also see the steadfastness of a bedbug
Why will I cry if I blossom in your eyes
like quickly spreading flowers, the ones which make
 everything beautiful.
Make me also forget about heartache and everything that
 is bad
with your love which surpasses everyone else's
the one which is broad and deep
which is sweet surpassing all fountains

Ewu! I am thirsty for it in a way that surpasses everything
 else
indeed I see that I deserve it!

Wherever I am I will remember it and be happy for it
your love which I have never felt in this world.
mother who gave birth to me disappeared behind the
 mountain and my father has passed on
My trust remains with you thus I do not want silver or
 gold
But if you are there I will be complete and I too will have
 a name.
The day I will see you I shall feel your love and know
my love ours will be the land of no hardships
What remains is that we unite, your place has long been
 prepared
The love within me is full and overspilling waiting for that
 day
when you will open the gates of my heart
The gifts you will be holding I will meet in your heart
Just imagine the joy and the celebrations that await us!

*Translated from the Zulu original – Zandile Khumalo's Ngenze
Nami Ngizigqaje – by Dr Innocentia Jabulisile Mhlambi*

FATSHE LAKA KGUTLELA HAE

Sesotho

Ke amohwawena ka dikgoka
Ha ke kopa o kgutlele ho nna
ke bulellwa hore kea hlopha
ke ballwa ditshito le melato
ke hlomakakwa dipotso
tse senang thuso
Ke a theosa ke a nyolosa
ha hona moputso
Kere ho hlolehile le ona mmuso
Ba re ba tla nneha lefatshe
Empa ke tla le etsang

Ke matha mantsweng a ntate Sobukwe
Lefatshe ke la bo rona
Ha le kgutlele matsohong a rona

Ba nkileng lefatshe ka dikgoka
ba re ba tla lokolla lefatshe
ka morao ha lemo tse lekgolo
Ha feela ba ka etsa serapa sa diphoofolo
Nna ka mona ke nwa metsi le diphoofolo
Ke phela jwaloka phoofolo
Ha bona ka mona ba etsa tjhelete ka serapa sa diphoofolo

Lefatshe kgutla re a ho hloka
wena o wa rona
re a ho hloka
Bontatemoholo ba re sietse wena
Empa ba di tlhotlhorile kgomo tsa bona
Ba re di ngata haholo di qeta jwang

Kajeno ha re na le ha ele nngwe

Lefatshe re o sebeditse dilemolemo
O orelletse mofuthu wa matsoho a rona
re o kgotha,
re o hlaola,
re o lema,
re fepa ditjhabatjhaba
Kajeno matsoho a rona a bolawa ke bodutu
Mofuthu wa ona oa kokobela
Lefatshe o se o hloname
Mobu wa hao ose o le theko e boima
Ho ya ka matlong ke ditjeho tse boima
Beng ba lefatshe ba hana ho re bulela
Re kene re bue le bafatshe
Ba re kgella fashe ka la rona lefatshe
Ba re kwalla ka ntle
Ha ba batle re pate,
re phahle
re leme,
re rue
le hore re hlabe
Lefatshe le hana ho kgutlela ho rona
Le ha puso ele matsohong a rona

Lefatshe kgutlela hae o hodile

      THABISO TSIETSI LAKAJOE

MAYIBUYE

You get violently taken away from me
When I request you return
I'm told I am nagging you
I am reminded about my crimes and trespasses
    I'm asked unhelpful questions
I go up and down
    with no rewards
Even the government failed
They say they will give me back my land
What will I do with it

I follow the words of Sobukwe
The land is ours
It must return to our hands

Those who took it through violence
say they will release the land
    after a hundred years
If only they can build a nature reserve
While I share water with animals
I live like an animal
While they make money from a nature reserve

The land is ours please return to us
    You are ours
    We need you
Our foreparents left you as our heritage
Their decimated their cattle
Saying they are plenty they deplete the grass
Today we don't even have one left

We have worked you for many-many years
You marvelled in the warmth of our hands
We digging you
We tilling you
We ploughing you
Us feeding nations out of you
Today our hands are lonely
Their warmth is getting cold
Your head is bowed
Your soil is now expensive
We can't even visit your graves
Owners of land refuse us entry
To enter and talk to our ancestors
They look down at us for our own land
They shut us out
They don't want us to bury
To intercede
To plough
To keep livestock
To shed blood
The land refuses to return to us
Even though we are government

Land return to us, you are now grown

Translated from the Sotho original – Thabiso Tsietsi Lakajoe's
Fatshe laka kgutlela hae – by Goodenough Mashego

O MPHOQILE KE O TSHEPILE

Sesotho

Ha maebakgorwana a ne a ka bua,
a ne a tla ntolokela a mpakele ka rato la rona la sebabole ka
 teng.
A llele matsapa, mahlahahlaha le matla a ona ho fetisa
 melaetsa nyene ka teng masiu le matshehare.
A ne a tla bolela ka moo a ileng a kenella mefuta yohle ya
 dipula ka teng,
Tse maru a thwathwaretsang, a tetemisang makwala ka
 teng ka dimpeng
Tsa Medupi, mefuta yohle ya dipula, ka ha ke mahlopha a
 senya.

Ya pelo e la kang ya tsietswa ke lerato
La mo ranthanya, la mo putula, la mo kgimula la ba la
 moswahlamanya.
O sa la a bua se tshwanang le se tswang molomong wa ka,
O mphoqile ke o tshepile
Ka metopa e toma ya lerato, o ntse a habea a re
O mphoqile ke o tshepile!

Le hoja se na se ntabola pelo, se nhodisa ka boima, se
 nlahlisa monahano,
Ke tshwanela ho se bua. ke se ntshe hobane tjhaba se so se
 ya timela.
Ke se behe poaneng hobane pinyane e nqeta nyene
 motshehare le bosiu
O mphoqile ke o tshepile.
Le hoja ke o teketse tsohle tsa rato laka le fetileng,
O entse tsona tseo wa ba wa feta.
Wa hlola waba wa pasela,

Ka hopola mantswe a mme a re rato ha le yo fatsheng lena
le ka kwano.
Ke ikwahlahela tsohle!
Nako ya ka eo ke e tsetetseng ratong le na le ntliseditseng
mahloko,
Le ntlhekefeditseng ka le tjhabang le le dikelang.
Leo ke qetetseng ke iputsitse hore o anyanese kapa o
motho nang,
Hobane hobeng haufi le wena... ho nkgofotse mahlo
Ka qhitsa ka le tjhabang le le dikelang.
Ke llela nako le lerato feela.
Hodima tsohle tseo ke o etseditseng ke llela nako le lerato
laka tseo ke di sentseng ho wena.

Setjhaba nnete se tshwanela ho e tseba,
O mphoqile ke o tshepile.
Ha ra tsohle le bohle bao ke nahanneng ba ka ntlhanohela.
Le hoja o itse o keke wa ho etsa,
O nranthantse, wa mpetlenya jwalo ka tapole e tjhesang,
wa lahlela pelo ya ka fatshe.
E sakgamane. Ho re ho bua tsena hotla nthusa... ke tla
bona.

Ke ntsha dinnete ke batla ho o leballa
O itse ke kgale ke le hokae ha o ne o utliswa bohloko,
Ka hlokofala ka lakatsa hore nkabe ke ile ka o tseba pele
batudi ba ka etsa,
Ba ka ntshenyetsa wena.
Wa kgutla wa re ke morati ya o ratang, empa bona!
Ho oka seso ka makgapha ho ke ke ha ntshebeletsa ha jwale.

Ke bile teng matsatsing a boima,
Ka o rata ha o ne o hloka ho ratwa, ka o tshehetsa ha o ne
    o thekesela,
Ka o fa matsapa ha o ne o thatafallwa
Ka o rata, e... ka o rata.
Ka inehela ho wena, ka itlama.
Ka qwela ke sa hula moya ka qhwelwa,
Ka o leballa,
Ka o tshehetsa,
Ka o rorisa,
Ka o kgothatsa,
Ka o neha lebaka wa phela,
Ka o lukisa wa ntlotla.
Hara mantswe wa re o tla dula, o tla nteballa, o tla
    ntshwarela,
Empa ke mona...
Ke mong, ke setse le nna eo a sa kang a tloha a mphoqile
A sa kang a etsa dikano meralo e so thehwe.

Ke nya matsete ke batla ho o leballa, o mphoqile!
Ke o tshepile le hona, ke radile ebile ke itse ke tla ba
    hlooho putswa ke tsofala le wena.
Ka o hlophisa, ka o beha ka manane.
Kgathe o leetong.
Ka o lukisa wa itlhola!

Hoba le tse tekenetsweng dikano di ya kwenehelwa,
Wa hla wa matha la ntshwekga hoba tsa rona e ne ele tsa
    molomo.
O ntshile ke sena tshepo leratong, o ntshentse.

Ba hlotseng jwalo ka wena bare o nkuketseng, o nkamohile
   eng, o ntlhokisitse eng.
Serithi sa ka, rato la ka, tshepo yaka, le bokamoso baka.
Le hoja o mphoqile, le na lona le qeba le keke la fola.
Le tibile jwalo ka kwetsa hantle.
Le qhomane ya ho ruthutha ntle ho qenehelo dibakeng, e
   ka kwano ho wena.

O lehuhudi le nhoholetseng tsohle tse mphethahatsang,
   tse mpopang, tse nketsang motho ya phethahetseng.
E la re batjho ba re mofuta ha o nkgwe ka nko e se qoba la
   kwae.
O mphoqile
Utlwa se na o mphoqile!
Ke tshepa o tla nka dikgudiso tsohle tseo tsaka ho hudisa
   eo o thetsanang le yena ha jwale.
Nke se o lakalletse thabo le lerato o nkamohile tsona,
Ba halefileng bao ke iphumanang ke le mokgatlong o le
   mong le bona ba re ha e ye! Le pele di na le baji.
Ka hona tseba, ha jwale ke haketse le pele di na le baji
O mphoqile ke o tshepile.

GEORGE THABISO LESEBA

YOU BETRAYED MY TRUST

If doves could speak.
They would witness and testify to our flaming love.
And decry their efforts, vigor and their power to send messages at any time of the day.
They would speak about how they penetrated various rains.
Thunderstorms that scare cowards and the bravest of men.
Torrential rains, all types of rains, since they are a mixed blessing.

An envious heart gets deceived by love
It struck him, devastated him and even destroyed him.
He remained speaking something similar to what emanates from my mouth
You betrayed my trust
With memories of love, he still declares
You have betrayed my trust!

Even though this tears my heart, places a heavy load on me, and blows my mind,
I must speak it and spit it out because my nation is vanishing.
Put it in the open as it consumes me day and night
You betrayed my trust.
Even though I shared with you all about my lost love
You did all those and outdid yourself.
You cast a spell and went beyond witchcraft
I remember my mom saying there's no love in this world.
I am used to everything
My time which I invested in this relationship that only

brought me pain.
That abused me when the sun rose and when it set!
That ended with me asking myself if you are a human being or an onion.
Because being close to you, hurt my eyes.
I descend when it rises and when it sets.
I cry only for time and love
Of all the things I did for you I only cry for my time and love which I wasted on you.
People deserve to know the truth,
You betrayed my trust,
Of all those I thought would turn on me
Even though you know good, you won't do it.
You trashed and destroyed me like a hot potato, my heart you dropped to the ground, it's still in shock.
Whether opening up will help me I will live to see.

I am spilling the beans so I can forgive you,
You said it's been long, where have I been when you felt pain.
I suffered and wished I knew you before the evil did.
Before they negatively influenced you,
You returned and said I am a lover. But lo and behold!
To treat my wound with shame won't work for me now.

I was there during difficult times
Loved you when no one did, supported you when you were shaking,
Gave you opportunities when you experienced difficulties,
I loved you... loved you,

Surrendered and committed to you,
I dived without caution and drowned,
Forgave you,
Listened to you,
Praised you,
Comforted you,
Gave you a reason to live,
Made good of you and gained your praise,
You said you will stay, forgive me, accept my apology,
Here we are…
I'm alone, remaining with the one who will never betray me
Who never made short-sighted vows.

I reveal secrets, I want to forgive you, you betrayed me!
I trusted you, I thought you and I would get old together
Take care of you, lay you down to sleep.
I didn't know you were just passing by.

Even vows can be revoked.
You escaped for ours were only verbal,
You left me with no trust in love, you tore me down.

Victorious ones like you say why did you lift me, what did you take from me, what did you deny me,
My dignity, my love, my hope and my future.
Even though you disappointed me, this wound will never heal.
It's deep.
Even rain that destroys without pity is on your side.

You are the floods that swept all that completes me, that
> build me, that make me a complete human being.

They say you can't judge a book by its cover,
You disappointed me,
Listen to me, you disappointed me.
I hope you will take all my pasture and feed whoever you
> are seeing right now.

As you rush to be happy and fall in love again you took
> them away from me.

Those I am in the company of say I should let you go!
> The future is uncertain.

Know that what goes around goes around.
You betrayed my trust.

Translated from the Sesotho original – George Thabiso Leseba's O Mphoqile Ke O Tshepile – by Goodenough Mashego

ESCAPE

ENGLISH

Next to her grandma
she is the daughter that swallowed rain and lightning
and still lived

Next to the wall
she is a corner safe
from any flood

Next to herself
she is a paddle on the floor
almost not there

BUSISIWE MAHLANGU

SCRAPS

English

I know about the taking having nothing does
and poverty that drowns a name
and replaces it with begging
and hands that are strong enough to overturn the world
but they are full of grease from fixing falling things

I was born in a place where people mourn lost jobs
like sons who die

follow them in the mud

and beg the grave to swallow them full

The weight of breathing in a body is rocks tumbling on
    shoulders
losing a job is dignity blowing out of a body
leaving dirt that water cannot wash away

finding a job is finding a slaughterhouse

loss has hands and legs and a pulse
loss is the number of heads next to a burning tyre
loss has a bullet in its chest

The country forgets to apologise for the shooting

sometimes we apologise for the protest and the smoke
we have to apologise for speaking

this is the place we never leave

                        BUSISIWE MAHLANGU

PHELO BJA LEHONO

SEPEDI

Thai! Kobo ya mme le tate di phuthetše mararankodi –
Dikgotsiša ba sa bonego.
Ke mantlwantlwane, bophelo bo ketwa boka diketo.
Phelwana bja boithatelo,
Phelwana bja go hloka bagologolo.
Phelwana bja go ipuša.

Diila ga di tsebje, ke sebjalebjale.
Dika le diema di tsene ka monga wa seloko.
Go anegwa ga dinonwane ke bogoboga –
Tšhalelanthago, ke ra hlola bja lehono.
Ke semphetekegofete, go tšerwe manoga le šele.

Mongwe le mongwe o itebeletše.
E ikabetše maphelo a batho tšhelete,
E laola diphedi tšhelete.
Tlhompho e nyametše boka phoka ge e hlabelwa ke
    letšatši.
Batswadi ke dikgapamamina, ke dithaka bohle.

Bana tsebe ga ba natšo, batswadi ba gogwagogwa ka dinko.
Dintwa le ditshele ke tlwaelo,
Marumo batho ba dula ba itlhamile,
Ba itlhamile ba letetše go kwa iiuu!
Ba agilego malapa mengwaga ye lekgolo,
Ba šupana tsela, thabo la gopa.

A ruriruri ke phelwana mang bja go bolaya malapa?
Motho o ja motho, mpša e ja mpša.
Malwetši a ikgašitše, fase le metša bohle.
Dinotagi le diokobatši, ke dijo tša bafsa.
Bohodu, bootswa le dipolayano ke bogobe bja ka mehla.
Ruri phelwana bja lehono bo inyefotše.

Feela ga go kgotsiše, pukukgethwa e re hlabetše mokgoši,
Ya re lootšang marumo, fase le tlo ema ka maoto.
La befelwa, la ahlama!
La metša bohle!

                        TSHEPISO MAKGOLOANE

IN LIFE TODAY

Thai! Kobo ya mme le tate di phuthetše mararankodi-
Only the blind are amazed
Life is treated like a game
People live as they please
A life without elders nor ancestors
Self-rule

These days nothing is taboo/sacred
We hear little of idioms and proverbs
Campfire tales have become an embarrassment
Regression, is what defines life today
It's competition, people are going astray

Everyone minds their own business
Money runs people's lives
It controls all living organisms
Respect dissipated like snow when the sun rises
Parents are disrespected, often treated like peers

Children no longer listen to parents, they are dragged left and right
Fights and jealousy are the norm
People are always armed
Armed to the teeth waiting for a scream!
Those who stayed together for tens of years
Are going separate ways as happiness dries up

What life is this that destroys families?
It's everyone for himself, dog eats dog
Diseases are everywhere, people get swallowed alive
Drugs and alcohol are staple food for the youth
Theft, adultery and murders are every day's diet
Indeed today's life has disregarded itself

But it's hardly surprising, the Holy has prophesied
That we should sharpen our spears, for the world will be
    in tenterhooks
Angry, mouth gaping!
Swallowing all!

Translated from the Sepedi original – Tshepiso Makgoloane's Phelo Bja Lehono / Bophelong Lehono – by Goodenough Mashego

BOKAMOSO BJA AFRIKA-BORWA
SEPEDI

Ke therešo kagi-kagi e a ikagela –
Tshenyi-tshenyi e a itshenyetša.
Bo kae bokamoso bja naga ya rena?
A ruri ke mang a ka ntšhupetšago bjona?
Ke kwele malobanyana, ge ba ntoma tsebe,
Ba re bo felela ka lebotlelong,

Lebotlelong la bjala, ka šupa letšatši!
Ke kwele maabane, ka pudi ya tsela,
Ba re bo metšwa ke diokobatši,
Ka latola, e le ka sekgalela.
Kganthe ba opile kgomo lenaka

Monamolomo ke mahlwa'dibona.
Lehono ke hlatse ya mahlo a ka.
Ke hwile kgaba, pelo e re tho-tho ka madi
Ge e bona tiro tša batho.
Ge e gopola tša maloba le maabane,

Ge e gopola madi a hlapišitšego Afrika-Borwa,
Ge e gopola ba amogilwego maphelo –
E le ge ba beakanyetša nna le wena.
Ke llela teng, mahloko a baka pelo,
Ge ke gopola mogolo gabo Afrika Borwa,

Feela humo le tlileng ka madi le ragwa ka maoto.
A ruri le reng le sa oketšwe?
Le reng le fokotšwa motsotso ka motsotso?
Ke phura marapo a hlogo ke ja di sa wele,
Mogopolo o šogašoga ntshesere,
Ntshesere nngalaba ya taba,
Gore balwedi ba maloba ba reng moo ba lego,
Ge thuto e hlokomologwa,
Thuto e se nago tefelo.
Ruri bokamoso bja Afrika Borwa
Bo gakanegile, bo hloka babetli.

        TSHEPISO MAKGOLOANE

SOUTH AFRICA'S FUTURE

A builder builds for self
A destroyer equally destroys for self
Where lies our country's future?
Who can show it to me?
I heard it through the grapevine
They said it drowns in a bottle of liqour

In a bottle of beer, I point to the sun!
I heard it through the grapevine yesterday
Saying it gets swallowed by drugs
I protested, it was in the afternoon
Indeed they hit the bull's eye

He who speaks has experience
Today I bear witness with my own eyes
I am numb, my heart sheds drops of blood
When it observes human behaviour
When it remembers days gone by

When it recalls blood that cleansed South Africa
When it remembers those whose lives were robbed
When they were preparing for you and I
I cry in silence, the pain gnaws my heart
When I remember an elder in South Africa

Wealth created from blood easily dissipates
Why is there nothing added to it?
Why does it shrink every minute?
I am restless, I can't even eat
My mind is struggling to process this

The elephant in the room is,
What are yesterday's fighters making of this,
When education is neglected
Free education
Indeed South Africa's future
Is confused, it has no visionaries

Translated from the Sepedi original – Tshepiso Makgoloane's Bokamoso Bja Afrika-Borwa – by Goodenough Mashego

ISIBELETHO

IsiZulu

Athi uKhulu Isibeletho somfazi
Sikuthwala konke.
Kuvundla inyoka, kuvundle ibululu
Siyamukela sibonge (X2)

Thina siyizintandane ezinhle ezikhothwa zimvula
Kwabona oNina asikaze sibabone.
Uma kusakhona uphahla lokufihla ikhanda
Siyabhiyoza thina sincome (X2)

Kwawona lamagxaba esiwagqokile
Yisibusiso,uyesabeka!
Asisakulambeli kwakudla,sesilambela ukusutha
Noma ikati eziko lingavundla kungabe kusadleka.
Sesikhulekela abazukulu,abantwana bethu
Kade babhunguka hleze izinseka sezaphelelwa
Nga mandla zanqundeka.

Nakhona emkhulekweni sesibulawa ngu valo
Kulezinsuku,
Hleze kwabona abazukulu bethu laba esibakhulekelayo
Bahlobise ngaphandle okwezibungu.
Hleze basathi 'Gogo,Gogo' nje kepha amathempeli
Sesingawaculela ngisho amagugu.

Athi uKhulu Isibeletho somfazi
Sikuthwala konke.
Kuvundla inyoka, kuvundle ibululu
Siyamukela sibonge (X2)

MBALI MALIMELA

THE WOMB

Grandmother says the Womb of a woman
Carries all
In it lies a snake, lies a puff adder
We accept and give praise (X2)

We are beautiful orphans licked by the rains
Even they have never seen their Mothers
If there is still a roof over their heads
We are joyous and full of praise (X2)

Even the tattered clothes that we are wearing
Are a blessing, you are awesome
We are no longer hungry for food, we are now hungry
    because we are full
Even if there is no food in the home and there is no longer
    need for eating
We now beg for our grandchildren, our children
It has been long since they left home even the pain of
    child birth
No longer has any bearing, they have been numbed.

Even in prayer we are scared to death
Perhaps even our grandchildren for whom we say prayers
Are beautifying the outside like worms
Perhaps they are saying 'Grandmother, Grandmother' but

the temples
Can now be sang a song about the possessions of this world
Grandmother says the Womb of a woman
Carries all
We accept and give praise (X2)

Translated from the Zulu original – Mbali Malimela's Isibeletho – by Dr Innocentia Jabulisile Mhlambi

NGIYAPHICA PHICA

IsiZulu

Bayok'hlekisa kuvele nelo mhlathi ongalazi
Bathi siluhlanga lunye
Siyafunga thina singabok'qina
Bayok'thela ngezinyembezi zengwenya
Buka! Bayok'dida

Bayok'mbambatha ehlombe
Ngemuva Bakhobobe, bayizitha
Inyoka iyothi isibuza nje iyobe isikade yakuxina

Ngaphandle bayak'teketisa
Ngaphakathi bayak'lwisa,
Baziqu zimbili ngyak'tshela bayasabisa.

Ngiyaphica phica.
Bayok'shayela ihlombe, bancome
Kanti kusangumkhakha weziqu
Zamehlo,'soke sibone'
Uyobe usuthi kuxabene ubendle
Kanti lutho belungekho kwaylona
Wena udidwa yisthombe.

MBALI MALIMELA

I HAVE A RIDDLE AND MY RIDDLE IS

I have a riddle and my riddle is
They are going to make you laugh until the molars are
 revealed
They are going to say we are one race/nation
We swear we are of the sterner stuff
They are going to pour crocodile tears over you
Look here! They are going to confuse you

They are going to pat you on the shoulder
Behind your back they sneak about, they are enemies
When the snake asks you, it will have cornered you a long
 time ago

In the outside they joke, infantilising you
In the inside they are fighting you
They are double-stemmed, I am telling they are fearful

I have a riddle and my riddle is
They are going to clap hands for you and praise you
But then it is just the phase of seeing and saying
"Wait we shall see"
You will say it is just a momentary misunderstanding
When in actual fact there was never any
You were just baffled by the picture

Translated from the Zulu original – Mbali Malimela's Ngiyaphica Phica – by Dr Innocentia Jabulisile Mhlambi

SLEEPLESS IN SOWETO

English

i. Every night's the same
Insomnia embraces me like an old friend
Tells me that sleep is for the faint-hearted
This is the truth that would haunt me in my dreams
If I could remember them at all
Instead, I lay awake with a pending darkness
That crawls beneath my skin

ii. I know it's there
The crickets seem to know it too
I hear them echo (and echo and echo)
Their secrets into the night and I pretend to do the same
Knowing deep down that my burdens are far too heavy
For this fragile skyline, or at least what's left of it anyways

iii. There's this park down the road
And I can sense its aura from here:
The synergy of a thousand blades of grass
All embracing the veld in its vastness
Jungle gyms made of swollen wood
And tyre swings occupied by ghosts of toddlers with
    splintered fingers
They're screams harmonious with the howl of rusting
    metal

iv. The trees outside are dancing
Moving to the random rhythm of resounding raindrops
The rhyme scheme runs repetitively
Rigorously resuming the revolution of reinforced religious
    beliefs

Rampant rumours raid rural minds as ruthless ringleaders reminisce
And sip sweet tea
In retrospect, these are the criminals I have been groomed to resent
But in reality, they are the only role models receiving respect

v. I have become somewhat accustomed
To losing this fight to my emotions
My character can only exhibit so much strength
Before my porcelain soul shatters inside
Where does the boy in me end,
And the man begin?

vi. Breathing should not be this difficult.

vii. Sleeping should not be this difficult.

viii. Nothing comes quite close
To the sting of toothpaste as my eyelid peels the fatigue off my iris
The smell of incense burning on the windowsill
As the morning explains itself to my cup of coffee
Prayer is the only thing that keeps the demons at bay
This is the mantra that begins most of my days.

ANGA MAMFANYA

CANCER

ENGLISH

mask your face in clay
procuress of your body
become a shadow

born from inferno
attempting to dissipate
ingesting the earth

the sand follows you
to the cascade in Howick
levitates your jump

sings Whitney Houston
drinking detergent
testing suicide

death captures you
cancer spreads from your bosom
solace comes at last.

SIBULELO MANAMATELA

IF WE WERE FOR SALE

English

if we were for sale
would you buy us happily with no complaint
and not care to check for any expiry date?
would you fall in love with us just by walking past our shelves?
would you buy us?

if we were for sale
would you underestimate our worth
and tell yourself that possessing us would be useless?
would you blow off the dust and dirt and still say you don't
see
beauty?

if we were for sale
would you complain to management about demand and supply and how the price is too high?
would you say you've seen the same thing on the streets
and nothing about us is really unique?

if we were for sale
would you buy us?

if we were for sale
would you respect us then because you paid for us?
would you love us because we cost too much?
would you know our worth because a tag says so?

would you?

would you ask for our manufacturers so you may tell them
to give the world us for free because we're essential?

if women were for sale
would you buy them?

TSHEDZA MASHAMBA

NGIYANILIBALELA

IsiNdebele

Nina beenhliziyo ezinoboya
Napheze nangithathela umoya
Nangitjhiya ngirabhalele
Nidlombana ningibulele
Ngiyanilibalela

Zisesebuhlungu iinyawo zami
Alikaphumi ivalo lami
Akasahlangani amathamb' ami
Kodwana ngez' aphel' amandlami
Ngiyanilibalela

Angikazonitjela bonyana zilungiseni
Begodu angithi kini rhubutjhekani
Nani zicabangeleni njengabantu
Iphasi nani lingelenu
Ngiyanilibalela

Yese nikhambe nenza
Nithandaze ningakhutjhwa
Niyifundisise niyazi ipilo
Benazi nokuthi inyawo alinapumulo
Ngiyanilibalela

BONGANI MASILELA

I FORGIVE YOU

You with cruel hearts
You nearly took my soul
You left me lying down
You thought I was dead
I forgive you

My feet are still sore
I am still frightened
My bones cannot come together
But I am still strong
I forgive you

I am not going to tell you to prepare yourselves
And I am not saying you must be humiliated
You must also think for yourselves
The earth belongs to you
I forgive you

You can just go and do
Just pray so that you are not taken out
Learn and know life fully
You knew that you might find yourselves here one day
I forgive you

Translated from the Ndebele original – Bongani Masilela's Ngiyanilibalela – by Dr Sponono Katjie Mahlangu

NNAHANELE

SESOTHO

A hao a peloa o ntshetsa kae?
Ke bolela ona mabinabina, dipatilweng
Tsona diphiri, makunutu a popota
A tswejwa ke wena, wena o nnotshi

Bang ha ba utlwa tsahao ba tsota;
Ba kgotsa kokgabane, boqhetseke;
Kebolela bona boqapi, bonono;
La haoleme o le ala phate.

Tsa hao dillo ke di tsebatswe!
Ke di tseba jwalokaha Mmopi a o tseba;
Ke tseba ho tshwenyeha, ho hlonama
Ke bolela ho nyakalla, ho thaba.

E ruri, ho robalake ho fetoha!
E ruri, tebohowena e a hlokwa!
Kajeno ke mehwabdi, kethaburane
Ke thaburantswe le ho harasanywa ke wena.

Maoba ho ne ho le monate o nyamatsete
A hao makunutu wa pepesa, wa beha pepene
Wa bua a pelo mabinana, dipatilweng
Athe rumo e kwetlile le lehohadi.

Ruri ho robala ke ho fetoha!
Wa kgoroha sa lesole ntweng
Wa mphenetha ntle le qenehelo
Aka maikutlo wa ila sekgethe.

Maoba o ne o tjha ntshi, o ikotlo sefuba
Kajeno ntho di fetohile, di senyehile
Ho wena ke fetohile sekgupi, kgupiso
Nnete ho wena e kae?

Ngwahola hlathe e ne e lelekisa tsebe;
Monakaladi o ja wa kebolelwa, o iketlile
Kejeno phokojwe e ngwaya ka nto lesele
Ha ke sa le mo tho, ke ntho esele.

Nnahanele le nna ke motho
Tsa ka ditokelo di se hatikelwe
Di hatikelwa ke mohlorisi, mmoloi
Wena mohloka-qenehelo nnahanele.

       AARON MPHO MASOWA

GIVE ME SOME THOUGHT

Where in you do you have neat shelves of secrets,
Where do you hide it so well from the weary eyes?
Your most dark, deep of them all are known to you,
And you alone are keeper.

When they hear about you,
They marvel at your name,
Your resilience and brilliance,
To create such art,
You only speak melody.

I have heard you cry,
I know you like the back of my hand,
I know and feel your suffering and despair,
I know your joy and happiness.

Change is for everyone,
Alas! How ungrateful can one be!
Today I am scarred, shattered to pieces
All of your making.

Yesterday was fun,
When you open up like a cracked nut,
Telling everyone with an ear to listen,
Sharing your deepest secrets,
A wolf in sheep's clothing.

Change is for everyone
You attacked like a soldier at war
Killing me without mercy,

My feelings mattered not to you.

Yesterday you were puffed up with pride
Today everything has changed, it is worse
I have become a provocation, an obstruction
Where lies the truth in you?

Yesterday was fun and games,
Living the dream within a sweet dream,
Today tables have turned,
I too have changed for the worse,
I am the monster created by you.

I am human too,
My rights should not be trampled upon,
They may mean a little to you my tormenter,
You are heartless and ruthless.

Translated from the Sotho original – Aaron Mpho Masowa's Nnahanele – by Goodenough Mashego

UMAKULINGANWE

IsiXhosa

Nywe, nywe, nywe
Uyakuva intsholo isitsho
Kuxokiselwana ngokuba siyalingana
Kaloku ukuvota kuthetha inkululeko nokulingana

Masithi kuyalinganwa eneneni
Kutheni kodwa ke ukuba kunjalo
Singathuthi sonke imigqomo
Singatshayeli sonke izitalato
    Hayi le yokuthi abanye babhetele
Ndivisiseni kakuhle
Nezinye iintlonga zasentshona maziphuphe ngesiNtu
Nazo mazibawele ukuba sithi
Ngezenzo nokuthetha
    Hayi le yethu yokumana sisithi umlungu mdala
Mna ndakuze ndikholwe xa bonke abahluphekayo
Behlala nathi ematyotyombeni nakwii-RDP
Kuvuke kukarajwe iintloko namanqina kudliwe iikota
Bambi babe ngonookhitshi onoogadi nonoogada

                ZONGEZILE MATSHOBA

EQUALITY

Whoa, whoa, whoa!
You hear such sounds.
People lie about being equal.
Voting means freedom and equality.

Let us say we are really equal!
If that is true, why can't we all collect dustbins?
Why can't we all clean the streets?
> *Instead of saying others are high flyers!*

Hear me clearly!
Even those from the West must dream about Africanism.
They must wish that they were black people!
In speech and activities!
> *Instead of saying a white man is experienced!*

I would be satisfied if all poor people
Live in RDP houses and in informal settlements.
As they wake up, they clean sheep's head and feet,
They all enjoy quarter-loaves of bread!
Others become domestic servants, gardeners and security
    guards!

*Translated from the Xhosa original – Zongezile Matshoba's
Umakulinganwe – by Angelinah Dazela*

UNGALONKULU

IsiXhosa

Uziv'unobungang'obungaphaya
Imel'epokothwen'ikwenz'ufun'ukuphalaz'igazi
Kukh'obawel'ubenz'imikrwelana nje
Bamb'ubawel'ubaqhawul'uqhoqhoqho
Usuk'apho inxeb'elinye kuphel'int'ebithethwa

Khawubethe ngalonkulu
Woyisiwe ziintonga weza noocelemba
Uza kugec'ezongal'ucand'ezontonga
Kukh'ofun'ubaqhawul'iintloko
Bamb'ubatyakatye ubacakaca babe ziziqwentshu

Uth'unyukele na ngalonkulu
Isinqe sikhukhumele lilah'elitshisayo
Ngoku ujong'uqhumfuza nezinj'ezi zikukhonkothayo
Uhamb'uxokhonx'udushe nje kub'ubawel'igazi
Uzikhusele wena hayi nosapho

Az'ukuba uva njani ngalonkulu
Njengokub'ushiyisana ngeencwina
Zezinkempe neembumbulu ezibangulwayo
Sele kudala waphulukana neliso de waf'icala
Hamb'uhambe ukhumbule kuyahlekwa kulogwala

ZONGEZILE MATSHOBA

THE HEFTY FIGHTER

You consider yourself a bully,
Knife in your pocket makes you thirsty for blood.
You are eager to stab people
You want to cut the others' throat!
One deep wound can take one's soul.

Please show us Big Bully!
You prefer a tomahawk to stick-fighting.
You will chop the arms as well as their legs.
You want to behead some of them
You have mutilated some of the bodies.

Are you feeling proud, Big Arms?
Is your waist swollen by burns?
You now aim to kill even the barking dogs.
You provoke everyone as you want to spill blood!
You protect only yourself and not your family.

I wonder how you feel 'Big Arms!'
Already you are groaning with pain.
Bullets and weapons are removed.
You lost your eye, and you are paralysed!
Remember that cowards are a laughing stock,
But families of heroes cry!

Translated from the Xhosa original – Zongezile Matshoba's
UNgalonkulu – by Angelinah Dazela

BA FOFILE

SEPEDI

Ba nyameletše ba bohlale ba Bohlabela
Ba fetotše Azania nku ya sehlabelo
Mašoboro a gafetše naga ganong la diphiri
Ruri naga e neetšwe ka baka la mogopo wa dinawa-
dikhwibidu

Re ba amogetše ka tše pedi
Ba re fetogetše wa tjontjobina madila a Sesotho
Ba re šia potla di hlanotšwe
Bodiidi bo re gomaretše

Bula mahlo ngwana wa Azania
Go reng o fetogile lesegafela
Reka pelo ya legakabje
Kgaitšedi ya seragamabje
O hlomole setšhaba mmutlwa
Naga ye ga se bogadi bja mmutla

KATISE MAWELA

THEY'RE GONE

The wise men of the east have disappeared
They turned Azania into a sacrificial lamb
Uncircumcised men handed the country to wolves
The land was betrayed for a bowl of lentil stew

We welcomed them with open hands
They turned us into fools and stabbed us in the back
They rob and leave us empty handed
Poverty trails us

Open your eyes child of Azania
Why have you become a laughing stock
Have a heart of stone
Sister to a sling
And rid the nation of its suffering
This country is not for games and comics

Translated from the Sepedi original – Katise Mawela's Ba Fofile – by Goodenough Mashego

SONDAE MIDDAE

AFRIKAANS

Sondae mag hulle nie fiets gery
of gebrei het nie,
want jy steek die breipen
in die Here se oog.

Die Here het nie omgegee
dat sy, wanneer almal dut,
gaan stap het nie – Hy het saam gestap
en "nee dankie" gesê vir almal
wat haar wou oplaai.

Hulle het lang en gevaarlike paaie
en draaie deur die proefplaas
en oor leë rugbyvelde gestap,
omkyk-omkyk soos 'n bidsprinkaan
wat sy prooi dophou.

Sy het vir Hom al hulle huisgeheime
vertel en Hy het niks gesê nie –
net geluister met oë
waarin 'n breipen gesteek is.

    MARTHE MCLOUD

SUNDAY AFTERNOONS

They were not allowed to bike
or knit on Sundays,
that pierced God's eye
with a knitting needle.

God didn't care
that she went on walks
while everyone was napping – He walked with her
and said "no thanks" to everyone
who wanted to pick her up.

They traversed long and dangerous roads
meandering through the experimental farm
and across empty rugby fields,
looking back like a praying mantis
eyeing his prey.

She told Him all their house secrets
and He didn't say anything –
only listened with eyes
pierced by a knitting needle.

Translated from the Afrikaans original – Marthe McLoud's Sondae Middae – by Pieter Odendaal

EVEREST

ENGLISH

Come with me into the barrens, the beating
heart of the raven-smutted sky.
Take my hand, as hard and knuckle white
as the dead men left up on Everest.

Crawl with me out of the torn tent
of our memory and tell me "I may be sometime"
while I hold only these lines. You loved something
    unlovable,
something hurt,

something unforgivable.
Then leave me, let the snow choke on our tracks.
There is no one to blame for this storm,
the earth is no witness, and winter leaves no fingerprints.

JANINE MILNE

HA RE ESO FIHLE

SESOTHO

Ha re tsebe "thuma mina" e fupereng,
E se e tletse hohle
Re hema yona, e nkga ho feta matekwane,
E nkga ho feta rajah e hadikang eiye,
Le dihenehene tsa ho jwetswa sefahlamahlo hore ke
    botsipasehole di a e tseba ena pina kajeno.

Morafo ha o kgore,
O metsa maAfrika a tshabe tshebetso,
Mmaene ke lebitla le dulang le ahlame,
Ho kwenya dikgutsana tsa batho ba Modimo.

Re se re tshaba ho ja,
Kota ya rona mafutsana e a fela
Ha ke sa bua ka French, nama ya rona,
Listeriosis, lefu le qabanya barui ka disutu tsa bona!

Beng ba rona ba kwenywa ke mmuso ka bo yona,
E ntseng Life esidimeni?
Re roma bo mang?
A le mong yena a ke ke a finyella.

Dibuka ha di fihle dikolong,
Bana ba wela ka matlwaneng dikolong,
Matitjhere a beta bana dikolong.
Bana ba fetohile dikgokgo, ka tlelapa titjhere e tsoha
    fatshe.

Ka mahafing ho kgwaetswe di-brown envelopes,
Mmuso wa Zuma o buletse mathata,

Tjhelete e jesanwa ke bona ba le bang,
Rona VAT e tlo re nyesa re se re ntse re nyele!

"You remaining data have depleted"
Yona ke molaetsa oo re phelang ka yona,
Le a tjhaba le a dikela inthanete e re tantsetse melala,
E ntse e tura ho ya pele,
Pele re tla roma mang?

Cape Town e otlwa ka lebaka la bokgopo ba makgowa,
Metsi ba a kgalla ba sa qete,
Ba utlwisisa tshotleho ya tlhaho,
Hobane le ya maiketsetso ha ba e tsebe.

Kerekeng ho tjhekwa tjhelete
Di ikeme tse bohata disatane,
Di qetella bofutsana ba habo rona,
Re hlohloreha sa diperekise tsa ho qetela difateng,
Diphokotho di a dutla.

Ho ho holo ke ho lwanela lefatshe,
La mang?
Ha re le nke keng?
Ho ho holo ke ho kgahlisa ka dipuo,
Diketso, sebono tsho!

Ha ke sa ikise ha ke rome motho,
Ha ke hloleha ho roma badimo ke masepa feela
Ha ke hloleha ho roma Modimo ke masepa feela.
Ho fihla teng ha re so fihle,
Ha ke tsebe re tla fihla na.

THABISO MOFOKENG

WE ARE NOT THERE YET

We don't know what "thuma mina" is all about,
It is all over
We breathe it, it smells heavier than ganja,
It smells more than an onion frying in Rajah powder,
Even idiots who get told to their face how dumb they are
 are familiar with this song.

Mines are never full,
It swallows Africans until they are scared of work,
Mines are an open grave,
Waiting to swallow God's poor souls.

We are now afraid to eat,
Our poor kota is running out
I don't even speak about French polony, our meat,
Listeriosis, death conflicts the wealthy with their suits!

Our people are swallowed by our very government,
What did Life Esidimeni do?
Who do we send?
He alone can't reach the destination.

Text books don't reach schools,
Children fall into pit toilets,
Teachers rape learners in school.
Learners have become beasts, they slap their teachers.

Under armpits they hide brown envelopes,
Zuma's government has unleashed problems,
Money is being shared amongst themselves,
VAT will hit us harder than we already are!

"Your remaining data has depleted"
Is the message we live by,
At sunrise and sunset the internet is strangling us,
It's more expensive than before,
Who shall we send to the front?

Cape Town is being punished for the sins of whites,
They crave water,
They understand natural disasters,
Because they don't even know intentions.

In church money changes hands
Wolves are hiding in sheep skin,
They complete our poverty,
We are being plucked bare

The most important thing is to fight for the land,
Whose land?
Why don't we take it back?
What's important now is to be content with rhetoric,
There's not going to be action!

If I'm not going I'm sending no one,
If I fail to send ancestors I'm nothing at all
If I fail to send God I am nothing at all.
We have not yet arrived,
I don't know if we will arrive.

Translated from the Sotho original – Thabiso Mofokeng's Ha Re Eso Fihle – by Goodenough Mashego

BOMENETŠA

SEPEDI

Ka kgonthe ya mmakgodi-a-kgokgo o tswetše o atile,
Lelemeng la digotlane o a hwenahwena,
Mebušo e tsogelana maatla, baetapele ba jana botala,
Dikgaruru re longwa tsebe, o hlobaboroko
O tšhilafaditše šedi, o bapotše kholofelo wa tswala
    kgakanego.

Baditšana ba tšwela pele ba dila go ithloboga,
Babuši le mantona ba kokomoga ge le hlaba le ge le dikela,
Serantlantla sa motsemogolo wa bomagoši se hlamula go
    feta wa go ja melatša,
Mebileng o a rena, o komangkanna
Kgorong tša tsheko o a ralala wena motswala
    tsogolekobong.

Mola etšwe mašemo a se nene o a rekiša,
O seganka o a ganka, le nthago ga o peke,
Ka nrago a go tswetšwe o mphenyašilo,
Re apere poifo, re golofaditšwe tshepo,
Naga e eme ka maoto e kgeregetšwe.

Naga e ya swa, e ya hulwa mohlodi ke wena,
Ga o na mohlodi o galakela dihlaya tša bohle,
Mmušo o gogagogwa ka nko,
O hlomile morako lefaseng la politiki.
Lelemeng la baetapele o tsokame,
Moropa go pidinya wa gago, re bina la gago lelopo,

Re mathasane, badikana ba koma ya gago
Go labalabela go aloga ga go re hole selo,
Ka mphatong re hlomile tsetsetse re tiela bošoro bja gago
   legoswi,
Mašoboro o a bolotša, bakgelogi o a kolobetša.

Lerumo la gago le bogalegale' a magala' a mabedi,
Tsela di pedi, ya gago ke e hlapa matsogo,
Diboledi di lapile go ratharatha ka wena,
Bomenetša ga o selo o fa ba bosenyi le bonokwane,
Ga ke go roge ke a go reta.

DANIEL MATSEPE MOHLALA

DISHONESTY

Truth is, you have born and multiplied
On the tongue of toddlers you whisper
Regimes declare war on each other, leaders betray each other
We get told about violence, you rob us of sleep
You muddied the situation and crucified hope to give birth to confusion

Poor people continue refusing to give up
Rulers and leaders get puffed up with pride as the sun rises and sets
The majestic palace capital of kings speaks louder than words
You are Lord of the road, boss of all bosses
In judicial courts you make rounds, you cousin of bribery

While we have few farms you still sell them,
You are a bully, you bully all without looking back
Son of your father you are a coward
We are afraid our hope is wounded
The land is under siege

The land is burning as you wipe off its flavour
You have no flavour, you are bitter to all who interact with you
Government is being dragged left and right
You have built a wall in the land of politics
You sit steady on tongues of leaders
We sing to your drum, we dance to your tune
We are initiates, in your initiation school

Looking forward to our graduation helps us with nothing
In initiation schools we are hopeless, we clap hands to
 your cruelty
You circumcise the uncircumcised, those who go astray
 you baptise

Your spear is sharp like a double-edged sword
There are two ways, I refuse to take yours
Speakers are tired of beating around the bush about you
Dishonesty you are nothing but crime and trickery
I'm not insulting but praising you

Translated from the Sepedi original – Daniel Matsepe Mohlala's Bomenetša – by Goodenough Mashego

MEGOKGO YA LEFASE

SEPEDI

Megokgo ya borutswana, bokotšwana, setshelanoka e
   tletše,
Mma nthuše sebanyabanya, selo se gana ke se bofa,
Ke megokgo e ya tsorotla, e ya runyarunya,
Ke' a gebelwa ke' a keketwa, ke' a lla ke' a golola.

Nthlomole mootlwa ga se mpue lenao,
Ke hlabilwe ka wa tshehlo tseleng, ee malalaakwaetše,
Šebešebe o seila, mmila o boima,
Tebetebeng ya leswiswi dihebehebe di ntshwela dihuba.

Aparela mongkobo, aperala mongkobo,
Tšeo ba di furaletše, ba godile ba ntsogetše maatla,
Mpunyane ba bolaile hlegere ba lebetše,
Ke tla šena meno a di nkgerekgerepe ka ba kwametša.

Ke tla ba swiela ka meetsefula boka mehleng ya Noah,
Bjalo ka kgabo ke tla ba latswalatswa lorelore,
Ke tla matloga ka bo gare ka ba meletše garegare maleng a
   ka; ka lalela,
Mahlong a ka ke tla ba fediša ka ikhutša.

DANIEL MATSEPE MOHLALA

TEARS OF THE WORLD

Tears of trials and tribulations can achieve great things,
Help me Mama, I can't restrain myself,
It's a torrent of aching tears,
I'm yelling, I'm yelping, I'm crying, I'm groaning.

Remove the thorn is not amputate my leg,
I was pierced by sharp thorns on the road, real ground thorns,
Peace you are alien, the road is tough,
In the belly of the night gossipers spit on my chest.

Do good to others, do good to others,
They have turned their backs on that, they have grown and turned on me,
They have forgotten where they come from,
I'll gnash my incisors and swallow them all.

I'll sweep them with floods like in the days of Noah,
I'll burn them to ashes like a raging flame,
I'll split into two and swallow them deep into my stomach; and lie in wait,
In my eyes I'll destroy them and rest.

Translated from the Sepedi original – Daniel Matsepe Mohlala's
Megokgo Ya Lefase – by Goodenough Mashego

EAT AROUND THE ROT

ENGLISH

Clear blue skies,
From a distance,
Birds swooping
And singing.
Closer to the earth,
The earthly scent of soil soothes
It has potential
To make us forget
And absorb our material woes.
Today as we traversed
A path walked by a thousand feet
My famished daughter
Bit an apple.
I looked at it.
She noted it.
The browning wasn't oxidation.
A little white slimy living creature
Born to the world
Ready for the soil.
She thought to throw the apple away.
I told her;
'No. Otla baka tshotleho?'
Just eat around the rot.

DIKELEDI MOKOENA

THE BRIDGE

ENGLISH

*My Grandmother   guide who lives between
my shoulder wings.*

i stick my fingers into the night,
pull them out, tips stained with velvet;

you come to me out of a crackling bluish-summer,
the open tongues of impepho the obsidian bridge.

between this world and the next – the slit
in the veil. curling air tenses, holds back the

dawn, suspends stars, and waits for you
to Speak. i have come   miles
out from the fog of the city,   skeleton
dreams limping under bright neon lights

to rest my knees before you, in the red soil
under the acacia tree, your daughter's eye
holding the leaf, the shadow of your son
holding the root.

Ke siametse go ithuta, Koko.

I am ready.

MJELE MSIMANG

THE THINGS I FOUND IN THE FIRE
ENGLISH

i write this naked, having opened my ribs and thighs
for the second time tonight to the thought of men

creating flames in each other's mouths,
illuminating the room in shadows that ricochet

off the walls, splintering the floors in sweat-shaped
bullets. how they burn themselves back to living:

the arch the sound of timber being licked open
by fire, the ash catching on the curling hair

on my nipples. my leg trickles light; somewhere in me, a
door unlocks to a shuddering spring dressed in a
    glistening

like mine; it turns, runs through me, shattering moans
    that burst
from the earth against the mouth. i cum, again, in the
    time

of a blade held against a throat for loving the unforgivable,
and i am held somewhere in a hand, now filled with
    honeyed

rain, given to reminding me of the flames that sometimes
keep me here, in this world, for a moment longer.

MJELE MSIMANG

NDZIMA N'WANANGA

XITSONGA

Ndzima, mahlo ya wena i lwandle ra nkhuluko lowu hi wu rivaleke. Nkhuluko wa ku haha ka maphaphatani na tinyenyana ta mihlovo yo pfumala mavito. Mpfumawulo wa switswotswana leswi nkekelaka swi khanela vusiku.

Tolweni hi xavisile misava eka vahundzi va ndlela lava hi tshembhiseke tilo. Tiko rin'wana ro xonga kule kule handle ka leri. Laha va nga tsheva hi kona malwandle i marhumbi ya vumunhu lebyi rhukaniweke. Tiko ra vakokwana ra ha ntonta ngati namuntlha.

Mahlo ya wena i lwandle n'wananga; leri eka rona hi tlutelaka eka vatolo lava hi va rivaleke. Vatolo lava hi va hlotaka emilorhweni ya vuhlangi lebyi longeke swa byona byi ngwingwa na vusiku. Tsundzuka Sankara, tsundzuka Biko, Lumumba, Cabral, na Guevara wa misava – xitshembhiso xa ndyelo ya nhlengelo na dzunde.

Tolweni hi nyikerile nsuku, namuntlha mati, mundzuku moya. Hambi mundzuku u ta dya yini. Hambi mundzuku u ta ya pfhomula kwihi – Nsami, Ritavi, na Xingwedzi i ndhope ntsena lowu fuhlekaka marhambu ya tihomu ta nkhwankhwa. Kumbexana wena a wu wa tiko leri. Kumbexana wena u ta aka vuxaka na xibakabaka.

Ndzima n'wananga; entsungeni wa xinambyana xa
Matlhwarhi, yi kona nsimu yi nga nava na ntsunga
kokwana Sikheto a nga ku siyela. Kumbexana u ta ya
pandza kona ya wena ndzima u hletela ntumbuluko, u
hletela ndzhaka, u hletela mundzuku.

Le Tripoli na Baghdad kurhula ku mitiwile hi tinhlori, leti
mbombometeke n'wayitelo wa vaaki endzeni ka
makwanga ya oyili. Hambikona mbilu yanga yi rilela
milorho leyi tlimbiweke hi cheleni. Milorho ya
kurhula, rirhandzu, ya leswi a ndzi swi tiva loko ndza
ha kasa ku kota wena.

Twana mimpfumawulo – Sona Jobarteh le Gambia, Feo
Gasy le Madagascar, Chalamanda eMalawi, Chiwoniso
eZimbabwe, Macuacua eMosambiki – kora, mbila na
xinari, swilombe swa rikwerhu. Kumbe yona yi nga ku
thova mapfalo. Loko a ri hina a hi phokotelela
N'warikapanyani. Kambe sweswi hi va
mphensamphensa wa doroba na musi. Hi va nkhuluko
wa lwandle leri leveke.

MOSES MTILENI

NDZIMA, MY CHILD

Ndzima, your eyes are like an ocean whose flow we have forgotten. The flow of butterflies and birds without names, the sound of small insects that are buzzing to celebrate night.

The day before yesterday we sold the land to passers-by who promised us the sky. A land more beautiful far far away, where they sailed, the oceans are a ruin of cursed humanity. The land of our forefathers drips blood.

Your eyes are an ocean my child. Inside which we sail into yesterdays that we have forgotten. Yesterdays we search for in dreams of a childhood that has gathered its bundles and departed with the night. Remember Sankara, Biko, Lumumba, Cabral, and Guevara of the soil – the promise of a pot prepared by a people.

Yesterday we gave away gold, today water, tomorrow air. What will you eat tomorrow, into what waters will you dive tomorrow? Nsami, Ritavi, and Xingwedzi are but muds that bury bones of cattle crumbling in the drought. Maybe you are not of this land, maybe you will find a home in the skies.

Ndzima, my child, above the small river of Matlhwarhi, there is a field unfolding on its banks that your grandmother Sikheto left for you. Maybe you will plant rows of your own to nurture nature, nurture your heritage, nurture tomorrow.

In Tripoli and Baghdad peace was swallowed by spies, who
drowned the smile of the people inside oil greed. Even
then my heart mourns the dreams suffocated by cents.
Dreams of peace, love, of things I knew when I still
crawled like you.

Listen to the sounds – Sona Jobarteh in Gambia, Feo
Gasy in Madagascar, Chalamanda in Malawi,
Chiwoniso in Zimbabwe, Macuacua in Mozambique –
kora, mbila and the string, our songbirds. Maybe they
can lend you comfort. As for us, we used to clap to the
dancing bird N'warikapanyani, but now we are of the
bustle of the city and of smoke. We are of the flow of
an ocean raging.

*Translated from the Xitsonga original – Moses Mtileni's Ndzima
N'wananga – by Aubrey Neo Sehlahla*

MKHOHLISI

IsiZulu

Ngokulalela umashaya ndawonye, ngakubuka ngakweya
Izelukeko ngazilibala, ngendelelo ngazishaya indiva
Inkece ngiyizingela, imigwaqo isiphenduke ikhaya
Izinqandamathe ngizishintsha, okwetshe lomnqakiswano
Kanti njengesela, uyofika ngingazelele
Ungizume njengegwala, njengob'thongo wangehlela
Watanasa ungamenyiwe, wenza umathanda
Usho ukungijuqa ungiqede, uhlasela nxazonke
Ngasala ngiciphiza izinyembezana, ngizibona ngiwohloka
Wajabula wayinqaba, washaya unqimphotho
Wangumlilo wequbula, wavutha phantsi
Waphenduka ubhememe, into engenakunqandwa

Bakubuke bakuxwaya, ugiya ungumakhonya
Usina uzibethela, ungenakuvinjwa
Kanti awuyifundanga yaphela, eyobuncwedi incwadi
Ngokuphazima kweso, ngakuphendukela ungalindele
Wadangala ngomzuzu, usudansela elami iculo

Ngakubona udumala, udikibala
Ungibona ngifulela ngezicubu, lapho usudlule khona
Namandla esebuya, nami sengivuka
Sengiqinaqina, nami sengizishayela
Sengihlome ngizingivolo, njengengane ngifundisiwe
Sengigadla nxazonke, ngamakhambi Nolwazi
Yize noma ekugcineni, kuyogcina wena
Kepha uyonginqoba usuzwile, nami ngikuququdile
Ngiyodlula sengibaxwayisile, abanengi ngawe

Kukhona abanengi ongeke wadlalela nakudlalela kubo
Abayokunqanda usavela, ongeke wabakhohlisa
Ngiyakholwa nosolwazi, bayobe sebenalo elakho ikhambi
Eliyokufica ungazelele, likushabalalise unomphela
Lapho uyophela unomphela, ngokuphelele

SIFISO MTSHALI

DECEIVER

By listening to the same old story I looked at you and
 undermined you
Good advises I forgot and in disrespect I ignored them
I hunted down money and the streets turned into a home
Lovers, I changed them so frequently as though they were
 a stone for competition
However, like a thief you will happen upon me unawares
You will come upon me subtly like a coward and like sleep
 you will befall upon me
You rejoiced uninvited and did as you liked
With an aim to cut me and finish me, attacking from all
 sides
I was left crying and I saw tears falling down
You rejoiced and even did a backflip
You became runaway fires, scorched down everything in
 your path
And you turned into a wild grass fire that could not be
 stopped

They looked on and were afraid as you danced
 authoritatively
Dancing with wild abandon as you could not be stopped
But then you have not read and mastered the intricacies of
 the book
Suddenly I turned against you when you least expected
You were disappointed when you had to dance for my
 song

I saw you disappointed and downcast
When you saw me layering new pieces where you had
    passed along
Power returned and I was also getting roused
Gradually getting stronger and I even began to strike
    myself
I am well armoured, like a child I have been taught
I am attacking with all medicines, Mother of knowledge
Though at the end you will eventually win
But you will win after a hard battle, after I have eroded
    you
I will go about warning everyone about you
There will be plenty of whom you will avoid completely
Who will stop you in your tracks and you will never
    deceive
I believe even the experts will by then have a remedy for
    you
Which will find you when you least expect it and
    annihilate you
Then you will be destroyed completely forever

*Translated from the Zulu original – Sifiso Mtshali's Mkhohlisi – by
Dr Innocentia Jabulisile Mhlambi*

BLACK OPHELIAS

English

Here we are
Living after all that has happened
Learning to build homes and ourselves
Hoping nobody will come tomorrow and unsettle us
We, people who go to the waters to find healing
While holding on to a great part of themselves
Because the waters have betrayed us before
Our bodies stay on the shores and we go to collect
    ourselves like shells
In all the souls the waters claimed and we weep with them
We weep in the freedom tides give us in coming and going

We celebrate by going to the beach to bath
In the waters of the well that keeps giving and taking
Enchanted with pearly-skinned girls who are there to
    swim
Here we are, confronting the world with ourselves
No, our deaths aren't suicides
Ophelia why do you drown yourself in springs
They drown us in our own skins and call it suicide
We can't swim because the waters might take us if we
    let go

                              SINASO MXAKAZA

DURBAN, 1986

ENGLISH

We trooped across the road to the beach,
that hot Durban night,
with a bottle of wine, not the first.
and a thirst for adventure.
Something to mark the night.
Strangers caught together
In a beachfront hotel after a seminar.

Who had the idea to dislodge it
from its lopsided authority?
That sign: Whites Only.
And so we wrestled it from its place
embedded in dark sand
and hoisted it high and carried it,
a sort of slow march to the shore,
and threw it into the sea.

It seemed defiant at the time.
Perhaps courageous.
But now I know it was not.
It was nothing.
Just a rusted sign thrown into the sea.

              PAMELA NEWHAM

LITTLE LOVE LETTER

ENGLISH

My uncle is dead.
Last night a knife was thrust into his heart.
The killer stabbed him repeatedly,
to ensure his instant death.
A Durban hostel killed a kind man in the night.
I miss his love and headlights.

Even as he cried, no one came to his rescue.
The drinking and the dancing continued,
as he lay down,
pleading and bleeding.
Even after he had died,
nobody cared to close his eyes.

This is my little love letter:
my final letter of demand.
Killer man,
bring back his blood
it is my lasting song,
to fortify our strong bond.

SANDILE NGIDI

BHEKI MSELEKU REGRETS YOU

English

When the place I now call home was barren land
And our fathers' fathers were only still learning to receive prayer
And sacrifice
And Rage
And song
There, in the years where black life was a rhetorical question
A thing to be left hanging
Without the necessity of answer
There, out of the abyss, emerges this
Train of men of song
Fleeing
And Mseleku's hand catching moments of stillness of sound
In flight
Gives anthem
Our brothers leave their limbs and lives in foreign soil
Mseleku's song is soundtrack to the mourning we are not afforded
His hands bring remedy
A place to call home
Until we no longer cry

A couple of limping decades after the false dawn
When we have forgotten our Selves,
Have lost the musicality of our names in the wind
He comes to find us
To find home. At last
But we have nothing left to give to him

No longer have use for the work of his hands
Can no longer create something of home for him
Can no longer arise and look within ourselves as he had
    taught us
No longer have arms
To cradle the weight of his weariness
And he dies
A death we don't quite know
How to mourn

BOMIKAZI NJOLOZA

STHANDWA SAM AFRIKA

IsiXhosa

Ubuze bobumnyama bakho
Bukhongozel' izothe lakho

Sthandwa sam Afrika
IsiNgesi nguMqeshi
Iilwimi zethu aziqeshi
Inkululeko yethu imbatshile
izwi elimhlophe liNOBUNGANGA
Elethu alinabunganga
iilwimi zethu zifuy' ihlazo
ezasemzini zinkcenkcesh' ulwazi

Sthandwa sam Afrika
Amehlo akho amfamekile
Umlomo wakho uhlafun' iingcinga
Iimpumlo zakho zijoj' ilize
Iintshiya zakho zingqengqile
Isilevu sakho sikhongz' iinyembezi
Imisebe yakho iphothene
Isibunzi sakho dikhongoz' ubukhovoka

Sthandwa sam Afrika
Thina ematyotyombeni, sidla khona
Emisebenzini, sihamba ze
Ebumnyameni, siyagwintana
Sityebe ngongabinanto
De sahlutha sanje, ngenxa yendlala

Sthandwa sam Afrika
Imali kuthi nguNongqawuse
Yona, iqelele okweqhinga leGqobhoka
Inqabe okwenqawe yegirha ebugqwirheni
Iqakatha iqelele iyogquzul' ukunqongophala
Amaxhala ethu axhomekeke ekuxakekeni
Iingxabano zethu zixhatshazwa lunxunguphalo
Siyaxabelana sixabane ngokuxhomekeka
Sixhomeke ngokuxhaphazana omuxhom' ixhala

Sthndwa sam Afrika
Izingqi zikaSolomon Plaatje zingumphunga
EzikaBiko ziyagodola
EzikaMandela ziyaqabaka
EzikaSobukhwe azikhwezeleki

Lala kakuhle ke Sthandwa sam Afrika
Ukhumbule ke –
Kokokuphupha kwakho akukho phupha limnyama
Sthandwa sam Afrika yam!!

        SIMPHIWE NOLUTSHUNGU

DEAREST AFRICA!

Your sheer darkness contains your disgust!
Dearest Africa, the English language is the employer.
African languages do not employ.
Our freedom is gloomy.
The white voice is BOSSY!
Our voice is just ignored.
Our languages consist of disgrace.
Foreign languages spread knowledge.

Dearest Africa, you are blind.
Your mouth is full of mumbling.
Your noses are no longer sharp.
Your eyebrows are just spread.
Tears fall into your chin.
Your eyelashes are twisted.
Your forehead accepts slavery.

Dearest Africa, we eat in squatter camps!
At workplaces we stay naked.
In darkness we assassinate each other!
Our wealth is equal to poverty!
Our stomachs are full of hunger.

Dearest Africa, we don't think of money.
To us wealth is UNATTAINABLE!
Money is scarce just like the pipe of a witch.
Money is far just like the 'BELIEVER'S WISDOM'
Our anxiety depends on our struggles.
Our disputes are influenced by anxiety.
We always fight because of interdependence.

We take advantage of each other!

Dearest Africa, Solomon Plaatje's footsteps have become vapour.
Biko's footsteps feel the cold.
Mandela's footsteps are full of snow.
Sobukhwe's footsteps can't make fire.

Sleep peacefully my dearest Africa.
Remember that your dreams are full of hope.
My beloved Country, my dearest Africa!

Translated from the Xhosa original – Simphiwe Nolutshungu's Sthandwa sam Afrika – by Angelinah Dazela

A SCENE AT GROOTE SCHUUR RES
ENGLISH

Feathers in tufts fall
    from a tree. They look like snow;
weightless, coming down slowly
            as a hawk works feverishly
on a pigeon's open chest.

           ZOLA NONGOGO

UNISA

IsiZulu

UJesu uthi: "Akekho oza
KuBaba ngaphandle kwami"
Ngiyasola wena uthi:
"Akekho oza kimi
Engedlulanga kuleli findo"

Abababele kuwe basuka kanyekanye
Kodwa kabafiki kanyekanye.
Abaludlana bathi pheshe bafike.
Abakhuluphele baphumula kabili.
Abanye baphumula kathathu.
Awubhenywa ungegudu lo mqansa.
Kwehl' izithukuthuku zibonwe ngamehlo.

Kwawakh' amagceke kushwez' obandayo.
Ngomzuzwana umjuluko uphenduk' izithukuthuku.
Ukukhathala kuba yinto yayizolo.
Abenzo abahambele lapho bayezwana.
Othamunda olukaMthaniya bayamuzw' abanye.
Okhuluma olukaMoshoeshoe bayamuzwa abanye.
Oveteza olukaQueen bayamuzwa abanye.

Asebebuya kuwe bayewukela.
Ungafunga badudulwa yinto.
Ubabona ngezithukuthuku ukuthi
Nabo bedlule kulo mqansa.
Bakhulumela phezulu.
Uhleko luqhuma phezulu.
Abebekuphokophelele kuwe bakuzuzile.

Wena uqhweba uwonkewonke.
Kuwena kuza zonke izinhlanga.
Kuwena kukhona abadala nabancane.
Bonke bavum' ingoma yempumelelo.
Abake baxhawula kuwe kabadeli,
Baphinda impinda kuhle kukamakoti.
Ongabaxhawulanga bahamba bajokole.

SIPHO ALBERT NTOMBELA

UNISA

Jesus said: "No one comes
through to the Father without me"
I suspect you have said:
"No one comes to me
Without having passed through this knot"

Those who want to come to you leave together
But do not arrive together
Those who are light-bodied just zoom by and arrive
    quickly
Those who are heavy-bodied take rests twice
Others take rests thrice
This steep is not smoked, it is not dagga
Sweat drips down and it is seen by the eyes

In your yard only the coldest air flows
In a few minutes sweat turns into heavy drops
Weariness becomes a thing of yesterday
The doers who visit there are in agreement
Those who speak isiZulu can be heard by others
Those who speak Sesotho can be heard by others
Those who speak English can be heard by others

Those who come from you are now across
You will swear something is pushing them from behind
You see by heavy sweat that
They too have gone past this steep
They speak aloud
Their laughter is high up loud
That which they intended to get from you they have got it

You signal to everyone
To you all the races come
In you there are young ones and old ones
All sing a song of success
Those that once shook your hands are never satisfied
They come back home again like a bride
Those whom you did not shake hands with walk away
    from you forever

*Translated from the Zulu original – Sipho Albert Ntombela's
UNISA – by Dr Innocentia Jabulisile Mhlambi*

MINA NGIYADIDEKA

IsiZulu

Mina ngiyadideka.
Mina sengiqal' ukuxakeka manje.
Ngixakwa yile ntando yeningi.
Ngobuning' abenzo baseKgutsong bakhulumile.
Idlanzana labaklami mingcele nalo lakhuluma.
Intando yeningi isotshozelwe ngeyedlanzana.

Mina ngiyadideka.
Saya phambili siya emuva
Say' eKhanana siy' eGibhithe.
EGibhithe kwakunje.
EKhanana kunje.

Uph' umehluko?

Mina ngiyadideka.
Imizi yabenzo iphenduke umlotha
Izimoto zabenzo zaba ngamalangabi.
Nal' ithayi lintantatheka nomlilo
Nakhu kuphamban' izinhlamvu zenjoloba.
Nas' isis' esikhalis' unyembezi.

Mina ngiyadideka.
Uph' uHulumeni wabantu?
Iph' intando yeningi?
Baph' abaholi besizwe
Cha, angish' ogcinalishone?
Izimpilo zabantu zisengcupheni.

        SIPHO ALBERT NTOMBELA

I AM CONFUSED

I am confused
I am beginning to wonder now
I am wondering about this will of the people
In numbers the doers of Khutsong have spoken
The few of the boundary makers have also spoken
The will of the people has been swallowed up by that of
    the few

I am confused
we are going forward, we are going backward
We are going to Canaan, we are going to Egypt
In Egypt it was like this
In Canaan it is this
Where is the difference?

I am confused
The houses of the doers have been turned to ashes
The cars of the doers are blazing flames
Here is a tyre running away with fire.
Here is a crossfire of rubber bullets
Here is the smoke from stun grenades

I am confused
Where is the Government of the people?
Where is the will of the people?
Where are the leaders of the people?

No, I am not referring to the window dressers
The lives of the people are at stake

Translated from the Zulu original – Sipho Albert Ntombela's Mina Ngiyadideka – by Dr Innocentia Jabulisile Mhlambi

LUFUNO A SI TSERERE

TSHIVENDA

Zwo thoma sa tshitori,
Nda nga ndi khou fhenda a Romeo na Juliet,
Nda omelela hanga muloro,
Mathina nda ndo digeda nga lo munwaho.

Na ntsia zwa nga tshitori,
Swiswini nda nga goswi,
Mato tshisima tsha zwililo,
Ndo fhaladza mithetho ndi tshi ndi fhanda tshi na muya.

Mbilu yanga ya dzhenwa nga vhupofu,
Nda vha bofu, nda kumba tshipofu,
Museto wo ndzhena matoni,
Lwanu lwo mpfudela.

Namusi ndi lila ndi ndothe,
No longa maswi a muhatu kha anga mato,
Lwanu lwo vhavha sa mazwilu magaga,
Mufunwa, lufuno asi tserere!

Matope thi tsha bika,
Ndode tshi tsha tha,
Phone ndi phorela.
Lwanu zwo kunda, sa muvhi uri a humele tadulu!

I la thase yanga...
Na thase a si mutshenzhe usina zwifhivhili,
Khe ndo shaya ndivho sa dodo?
Ngavhe ndi limuwe uri thase i a fhisa, a si ya tshedza
    fhedzi.

Tserere i a suvhisa, wa huvhala,
Lukunda a lu kokomedzwi, lu a thara,
Nama kombetshedzwa i a phula khali,
Nne ndo a thupha, tserere ndo lamba!

MUSHAYATHONI BRIDGET NWOVHE

LOVE IS NOT EASY

It all started as a story
Just like Romeo and Juliet,
It was like a dream,
I was relaxed.

And he left me like a story
I was left scared in the dark.
I kept crying,
My heart was in pain,
My heart was blinded.
I became blind and fell in love.
I felt the pain in my eyes.
Everything turned sour.

Today I am crying all by myself.
With no one to sooth me,
It is like you sprayed my eyes with the skin of an orange.
My love, love is not easy!
I am tired now.
I am no longer playing these games.
Am tired of crying over the phone,
Your love has defeated me, like a sinner who is reminded
   of heaven.

My queen...
My queen has turned into dirt.
Maybe I lacked wisdom like a fool?
I should have known that such beauty would kill me, looks
   are indeed deceiving.

Beauty, just like mud, can make you slip and get hurt.
You cannot force love, because if you do, it will kill you.
I have seen it all. (seeing is believing)
I give up, am done!

Translated from the Venda original – Mushayathoni Bridget Nwovhe's Lufuno A Si Tserere – by Aubrey Neo Sehlahla

HONDSEGEDAGTE

AFRIKAANS

Arme hond. Hy sluip hier rond terwyl ons
die brood moet breek. Hy beloer jou met
sy kop omlaag, die hond. Hy dink hy sal
'n krummel kry as dié ooit val, maar dis
verniet, die arme fokken hond. Dit klou
aan 'n nat vinger en rol op jou eie mond

Die brood moet breek, want ons is bleek
van honger. Arme hond. 'n Klontjie botter
is 'n droom vanuit 'n ander tyd, toe ons
nog almal jonger was, arme hond. Nou
breek ons die brood op, skraap dit in vet
van laasweek, al is dit ongesond

Arme hond. Hy grawe in die grond. Harde
bene om te kou, maar dit maak vir lekker
sop: Dun is die water, en as hy tjank, help
'n goed-gemikte skop, die arme hond.
Hy sluip eers weg, kom kruip dan terug,
reuke op sy snoet van ander stront

Hy lê by ons voete, die arme fokken
hond. Hy lek aan ons vingers, dit help
om hul skoon te hou. Hy druk sy snoet
onder jou hand in, die hond. Hy lek
aan sy pote, hy byt in sy lieste, jeuk en
byt en word een groot fokken wond

HANS PIENAAR

DOG THOUGHTS

Poor dog. He prowls about while we
must break the bread. He ogles you with
his head held low, this dog. He thinks he'll
scout a crumb that falls, but it's all
for nought, the poor fucking dog. It clings
to a wet finger, and into your mouth it rolls.

The bread must break, because we are pale
with hunger. Poor dog. A pat of butter's
a dream from another time, when we
were all younger, poor dog. Now we
break the bread apart, scrape it in last
week's fat, though it's quite unfit.

Poor dog. He's digging a hole. Hard
bones to chew, but they make tasty
soup: The water's thin, and when he whines,
a well-placed kick does the job, poor dog.
He cowers away, then cowers back,
his snout smells of other shit.

He lies at our feet, the poor fucking
dog. He licks our fingers, it keeps
them clean. He jostles his snout under
your hand for more, the dog. He licks
his paws, he bites his loins, itches and
bites and becomes one big fucking sore.

*Translated from the Afrikaans original – Hans Pienaar's
Hondsegedagte – by Pieter Odendaal*

BATJHA

SESOTHO

Batjha le ya kae le potlakile?
Ha lebone tsela empa tsatsi letjhabile.
Tshwarang letie le sa le tjhabetse,
Holang, lethenthetse le sa le tjhabetse.

Motjha nako e o file ona marapo,
Nako ya ho kgaba eseng ho robala malopo.
Tsetlallelang ho tswella le sa na le nako,
Le kgabeng pele le fetoha dithako.

Tsatsi ha le se tjhabe le sa paqame,
Hoba e tlang ke nako, e tla e palame,
Nako haena ena abuti kapa motswala,
Motjha tsoha e fihlile nako ya ho sela.

Motjha tlase lefatsheng mona o morumuwa,
Pheta ditaelo jwale ka yena mothoduwa.
Hoba nako le metsotso ya botjha ba motho,
Ha e kodumela e ba yona tshomo-ka-mathetho.

Telang timiti le tele le ona masawana,
Le be matjato a ho tsoha ka madungwane.
Tshwarang ka matla le sa tjhabile,
Ha le dikela o tsebe ho fedile.

Ha le dikela ohle o lebale,
Hobane ho kgutla ha le kgutle lekgale.
Lefatsheng lemo tsa botjha ba motho,
Dintle empa ha di kodumela eba ke phetho.

Motjha akga diala o tone mahlo,
Hoba le ka kwano le meutlwa le ditshehlo.
Le lekgonatha le batla motho a bohlale,
Kgaba ka mathata motjha obe seemahale.

        SEHLOHO PIET RAMPAI

GENERATION X

Generation X where are you going in such haste?
You don't see the way yet the sun is fully bright.
Be hands on when you still can,
Grow, have fun while the sun is still bright.

Generation X time has given you a chance,
Time to shine and don't go astray.
Strive while there is still time,
Succeed in excellence before all fades away.

Make means and efforts while you still can,
For the time will come, it's upon us.
Time knows no gender nor relation,
Generation X wake up and make it happen.

Generation X you are on Earth for a purpose,
Do your part as a bearer of good,
For the time of youth does fade away.
When the clock strikes so shall you.

Do away with senseless behavioural culture,
Be that early bird that catches the fat worm at dawn.
Hang on tight while you still can,
For the time is no longer on your side.

Lost time cannot be recovered,
Every second counts, can never be the same as the next.
Time is precious and should be cherished by all,
The fruits of youth should be cherished while ripe.

Generation X build that empire with your might,
For your path is narrow and full of thorns.
Be wise lest you be consumed by greed and envy,
Shine bright and be the legend.

Translated from the Sesotho original – Sehloho Piet Rampai's Batjha – by Goodenough Mashego

LABELS

ENGLISH

I am a positive nihilist.
A spectrophobic, autophobic, catastrophic thinker.
A heterosexual sapiosexual
With some bisexual leanings.
(Love me).

I am an atheistic Jewish girl,
So I think and write a lot.
I am an onychophagic, trypanophobic existentialist.
A follower of fashion from the 1980s
Attempting to be body positive.
(See me).

I am a socialist with a dash of practical capitalism,
An anti-classist semi-Marxist,
An anti-racist semi-artist,
A generally generous idealist
With some logical leanings.
(Hear me).

I am tired of labels.

JULIETTE ROSE-INNES

FAITH

ENGLISH

I am tear-stained and grass-stained
when she picks me up from school.
As I get into the car, I hide the graze on my elbow
but I relay word-for-word the details of the scrap.
How I defended their honour. Swore they'd never lie.
As we drive from the car park, I am a small fuming zealot.
Adamant. Declaiming. Undaunted.

An intervention is clearly necessary.
So, before she washes my face or feeds me lunch,
she takes me quietly straight from the car to the study,
shuts the door, holds my hands,
tells the truth.
There is no Father Christmas.

"He's really make-believe?"
"He's really make-believe."

I stare through the window as she talks on.
Out in the garden my little sister
draws her Miss Piggy muppet puppet by one leg
over the sun-filled lawn.
She's singing a tune she just made up.

I cry again but nod, agree.
We will keep up the pretence a little while longer, at home.
For her sake.

I look out at her as she hums over the flowerbeds.
She is happy and faraway on the other side of the glass.
But this will happen to her too.

In the weeks that follow, I double my scrutiny.
If they could lie about this?

This Jesus, then?
He can really hear them?
All my thoughts?

                              DEBORAH SEDDON

O SWELE MPHATO

SEPEDI

šo lehono o gapa tše tšhweu fela
hlogo e hupile morodi
o be a phemela naga bjalo ka mohlabani
mola bangwe ba hlwetše maaka le meratha

ke tate!
ditsebe ga di sa kwa
bošego ga a robale
o tshwenya ke sepoko
meno o šina a sa fetše
o re go bolela, a buše a ikarabe

mefoma ya angola le swaziland di mo onaditše
mokokotlo o gana go otlolloga
gago tema ntle le lehlotlo
mengwaga ke ye masomehlano
ruri ke tša batho!

meraba e a dutla
bana ba gomišwa dikolong
ka baka la mokitlana
go a pala
mphiwafela o a itatola boka ditaola
di šitile phaahle
ebile o gafa ntahle

aforika-borwa ye mpsha
e lokollotšwe bokgobeng
kgoro ya therešo le poelano e kgaotše tshele
koša re sa bina e tee

muši wa tokologo o sa foka
letswai nameng
legare phokeng

14 ya mengwaga robben-island
o ile a kgoketšwa ka diketane
a botoga direthe di palegile
ka malala-a-kwaetše
kgopolo e šila menatla
o bonetše bagale
ba re go galefa
ba mo gaya ntaka ka legare
ruri o di bone dikoma

lehono ba gorogile bagale/adi
bo mandela, sisulu, kathrada le bangwe
mmušo o ba hlakeletše ka diketekete
ge e le tate ya lešidi a hlokišwa
ge e le tše dingwe re boifa go di laodiša
re tšhaba baditi le meretlwa

a gona taba
ge e le koma e alogile
aforika-borwa ke ngwana yo a lokollotšwego popelong
e tswetšwe ka lefsa
yo a sa rego šatee, o a duma!

                        MOSES SELETISHA

THE INITIATION SCHOOL WENT UP IN FLAMES

Today you walk with difficulty
A bullet pierced your skull
You were protecting the country like a warrior
While others were lying and feasting

My father
He can no longer hear
He can't sleep at night
He has nightmares
He gnashes his teeth non-stop
He answers his own questions; talking to himself

caves in swaziland and angola damaged him
He cannot straighten his spine
He can't walk without a stick
He is only fifty
This is witchcraft!

He is broke
His children get evicted from schools
He cannot settle his debts
It's hopeless
He's too young for pension
No one helps him
He's losing his mind

New south africa
Has been freed from slavery
Truth and reconciliation commission ended hostilities
We are still singing the same song

There's still liberation smoke in the air
Peace
Relax

14 years on robben island
He was shackled in chains
arrived heels bleeding
Pierced by thorns
Your mind grinding
You saw secrets of warriors
When they got angry
They shaved his head with a razor
Indeed you saw dark secrets

today s/heroes have returned
mandela, sisulu, kathrada and others
government thanked them with thousands
while my father received nothing
we are afraid to relate other tales
we are afraid of what might come of us

it's fine
that you graduated from initiation
south africa is a child freed from the womb
has been born again
he who does not ululate is jealous

Translated from the Sepedi original – Moses Seletisha's O Swele Mphato – by Goodenough Mashego

HAZARDS

ENGLISH

We hold storms on our tongues,
Every day.

We walk past the streets like tornadoes,
Raging.

Our palates are wrathful skies,
Perplexed
thrusting our tongues to create lightning
in our mouth

Our gums are volcanic eruptions,
Shaking
ready to release the molten voice of our words

We overflow on everyone
as hot as we are;
always aimed to claim everything

We have drowned many of us
in rivers they sucked through their ears.

We layed mountains on tombstones,
for dreams
Never to wake up in calls of resurrection.

We are known for no good but destruction,
to turn our lives into hazards.

NKWANA JOSHUA SERUTLE

OBAB' ABANGEBABA

IsiZulu

Yaqonda ngqo kim' intokazi
Intokaz' owuwangafung' uth' uzime.
Yanyathela kabili kathathu maqede yamoyizela.
Yatshikizis' umzimba phambi kwami
Wen' owabon' onobuhle bekhiph' amakhono
Kimina kwaqubuk' uthand' olubabazekayo
Ngakhumbul' ukuthi ngake ngaba yinsizwa.
Cha, angikhuzelanga; sasingasekh' isidingo
Ngahlal' odabeni funa ngiphunyukwe yiqatha.

Yangithi laphalazi ngamehlo amhlophe qwa
Yashay' isikhwehlela yase ithi,
"Mina nginguNtombenhle
Ngizalwa kwaSokhela
NgingowakwaMkhiz' eMakhabeleni.
Laph' eGoli ngiziphilisa ngokuthengisa ngomzimba."
Kwashwaban' ulimi; ngakhuluma okuzwakalayo
    nokungezwakali
Yize kwafik' umqondo wokuthi ngiqhel' eduze kwayo,
Amahlon' angithi ngqi! Ngema phuhle!

Yaqhubeka yathi, "Ungazikhohlisi uthi ubona intombi
Min' angiyon' intombi,
Min' angikaze ngibe yintombi,
Min' angisoze ngaba yintombi
Noma ngabe ngifisa kangakanani,
Wen' ubon' umfanekiso wentombi
Min' obam' ubuntombi ngabephucwa ngobaba
Obab' abangebon' obaba ngoba bebaba.
Obab' ababezwana nomama bangidlwengula bephindelela."

Zagcwal' emehlweni' izinyembez' entokazini
Yaqale yazam' ukuzibamb' ngezinkophe
Ekugcineni zageleza ngemisedlan' emibili
Imisedlan' engafunda kwezami;
Yayidalwe yikh' ukuhlal' ikhala.
Yazesula yas' ithi, "Ngisengumntwan' angibonanga cala
Mina ngangithi yint' eyenziwa yibo bonk' obaba.
Langa limbe ngamazis' umama
Kwab' ukwehlukana kwabo."

Yaqhuba yathi, "Wamthol' umam' omuny' ubaba.
Kwaqala kwaba kuhle saba ngumndeni
Ubaba waqal' ukungithint' amabele
Lokhu wab' ekwenz' um' umam' engekho
Wayekwenza lokh' elandelisa ngamazwi,
Wayethi ngimuhle ngifana nomama
Njalo uma engibona ngangimkhumbuz' umama.
Angiwuvumelang' umqond' owawuth' angilubik' udaba."

Yaqhuba yathi, "Umshado kamama wokuqala wachithwa
    yimi
Umshado kamama wesibili wawuzochithwa yimi
Ubaba wayelala nami ngenkani mihla nezolo
Wayethembisa ukungibulala uma ngike ngathi vu.
Mina ngafa ngiphila; ngapoka ngiphila.
Ekugcineni ngasithath' isinqumo
Isinqum' esangehlukanisa nomama
Umam' engimthandayo; umama ozwana nabahlukumezi
Ngalifuthel' ikhay' elalingihlukumeza."

Ukuzibika kwam' okwavusel' intokaz' amanxeba
Kwaphazamiseka lapho kum' imoto kanokusho stopped by
Yama maqeda kwavulek' ifasitela lomshayeli.
Yathi jeq' intokazi yas' ivalelisa kimi.
Yathi, "Ngicela sehlukane yiklanyente lami lel' elimayo."
Angazanga noma kwakumele ngivalelise yini.
Ngama khimilili ngalubuk' unyanyavu lunyelela.
Ngesikade ngazizwa sengikhuluma ngedwa okohlanya,
"Yonk' int' eyenzekayo yenzeka ngesizathu."

                BUKELANI MMELLY SHANGASE

FATHERS WHO ARE NOT FATHERS

The lady came directly onto me
The lady that you would swear was a beauty pageant.
She stepped twice thrice and thereafter smiled
She swayed her body in front of me
As beauty pageants do
In me there grew rapidly the kind of love beyond description
I remembered that I once was a young man.
No I did not propose there was not need
I simply stated my matter as I did not want to miss this opportunity.

She eyed me with those extra white eyes
She cleared her throat and then she said,
"My name is Ntombenhle, The Beautiful one
I am a daughter of Sokhela
I am of the Mkhize clan from eMakhabeleni.
Here in Johannesburg, I survive through selling my body."
I was tongue-tied; what I said next made and did not make sense
Even though there was a nagging idea that I should stay away from here,
I was embarrassed to do so! I stood motionless!

She went on to say, "Don't fool yourself and think that you see a maiden;
I am not a maiden,
I have never been a maiden,
I will never be a maiden
Even though I can wish it with all my heart

You are only seeing an image of a maiden
My maidenhood was taken away from me by fathers
Fathers who were not fathers because they lacked integrity
Fathers who were in love with my mother raped me
    repeatedly."

Her eyes welled up with tears
She attempted to hold them back with her eyelashes
In the end they simply formed two furrows and flowed
    down
These furrows I learnt for myself;
Were formed by constant crying.
She wiped her tears off and said, "While still a child I did
    not see anything wrong
I thought this was what was done by all fathers.
One day I told mother about this
And that was their separation."

She continued and said, "Mother found another man.
Initially all was well. We were a family
Things went awry when I became an adolescent
Father started touching my breasts
He did this when mother was not around,
He usually did this and thereafter said
I am beautiful, I resemble my mother
That every time he sees me I remind him of my mother.
I did not agree with the idea that I should tell about this
    thing."

She went on to say "Mother's first marriage was ruined by

me
And mother's second marriage will also be ruined by me
Father had sex with me forcefully frequently
He promised to kill me if I said anything.
I died alive and haunted alive
In the end I took a decision
A decision that separated me from mother
The mother I love, the mother who loves rapists
I turned my back from a home that was molesting me."

It is my talk about love to her that dug up wounds in the young lady
The conversation was disrupted when a flashy car stopped by
It stopped and then the driver's window was opened.
The lady took one look and bid me farewell.
And said, "I bid you to go, this is my client that has just stopped."
I did not know whether I had to bid her farewell too.
I stood fixed at a spot as I looked on as the flashy car slowly drove away.
After a long pause I heard myself talking alone like a mad man,
"Everything that happens, does so because of a reason."

Translated from the Zulu original – Bukelani Mmelly Shangase's Obab' Abangebaba – by Dr Innocentia Jabulisile Mhlambi

KONAKELEPHI?

IsiZulu

Zehla kwamanz' izifuba kwabesifazane
Kwashintsh' amath' emilonyen' ababa ha
Bakhihl' esikaNandi ngezwe lokhokho
Izwe lokhokh' elalisosizini lwengcindezelo
Sasisikhul' isililo somame besililo.
Ulaka lwalubhalw' emehlwen' emadodeni
Izingane zazishesha emigwaqweni
Kukhona okwakumele kulungisiwe.
Sekwedlule lokh' sesikhululekile
Inyamazane seyibanjiwe kumele yabiwe
Esikhundleni sokuthi yabiwe ngononina
Silibel' ukubhekana ngeziqu zamehlo.
Siyahamb' isikhath' asimele thina
Siyogcin' ngokuyidla ngephunga.

BUKELANI MMELLY SHANGASE

WHERE DID IT GO WRONG?

Chests fell like rain among women
Saliva changed in the mouth and became bitter
There was an outcry – just as when the Zulus cried at
    Nandi's death – about the land of our ancestors
The land of our ancestors which at one time was besieged
    by suppression
The outcry was loud, the outcry from mothers' unions
Anger was written on the eyes of the men
Children were walking fast on the streets
There was something that needed to be corrected
That has gone past now we are now free
The game has been caught it must be shared
Instead of it being shared equally amongst everyone
We are now glaring at each other in evil ways
While time passes by without waiting for us
We will eventually only smell the flavours

Translated from the Zulu original – Bukelani Mmelly Shangase's Konakelephi? – by Dr Innocentia Jabulisile Mhlambi

IZIZUKULWANE

IsiZulu

Ukhokho wakhononda ngomkhulu,
Umkhulu wakhononda ngobaba;
Ubab' uyakhononda ngami.
Ubab' uth' akaphendulwa yingane
Asekushilo yena kumele kwenziwe.
Kanti konakala kusiphi isizukulwane?
Isizukulwane ngasinye sisol' esisilandelayo?
Kumele kulungiswen' ukuze kulunge?

Mina ngibon' ikusas' eliqhakazile;
Abangikhulisayo bathi bayoyicel' ivuthiwe
Engikwenzay' abangikhulisayo abakuthandi
Bathi bona babengenzi njengami,
Bathi bona babebahlonipha abazali babo,
Bathi min' angibahloniphi bona,
Bathi mina ngifun' izizathu zabakushoyo,
Bathi mina ngilalel' abangani kakhulu.

Kanti nguban' okumele ngimlalele?
Kanti lincike kuban' ikusasa lami?
Kanti nguban' owazi ngekusasa lami?
Abangikhulisayo bayakwaz' okwayizolo;
Abangikhulisay' abakwaz' okwakusasa;
Okwayizol' akufani nokwakusasa.
Kant' uban' owaz' okumele kwenziwe
Ukuze kuhlangatshezwane nekusasa?

Bazali bethu sikhululeni sizibonele;
Enisihlelela khon' akukhon' okungasiphilisa
Isikhathi sethu sehlukile kwesenu,

Ngezikhathi zenu nanifuy' ochibidolo;
Namuhl' abelusi basezikolweni.
Nina nanibuk' omakhelwane ngokwemizi;
Thina sibabuka ngokwamazwe omhlaba.
Eleth' ikusasa liqhazile kunelenu

BUKELANI MMELLY SHANGASE

GENERATIONS

The great-grandparents complained about grandfather.
Grandfather complained about father;
Father complains about me.
Father says a child does not talk back to him
His word is final and should be followed.
But where did it start to go wrong, generationally?
Each generation blames the one which comes next?
What must be fixed so that things are set right?

I see a future that is bright;
Those rearing me up say, they are not sure, they are sceptical.
What I do those that are rearing me up do not like
They say they did not do things the way I do.
They say they respected their own parents.
They say I do not respect them.
They say I am looking for reasons for what they say.
They say I listen to friends too much.

But who must I listen to?
But to whom is my future dependent on?
But who knows about my future?
Those rearing me up know about yesterday;
Those rearing me up do not know about tomorrow;
Things of yesterday are not similar to that of tomorrow
But who should know what is to be done
So that tomorrow is anticipated?

Parents set us free so that we see for ourselves;
What you have planned for us is not what can make us

live.
Our time is different from your time,
In your time you kept livestock aplenty;
Today the herders are at school.
You looked at neighbours in terms of nearby surrounding houses;
We look at neighbours in terms of countries of the world.
Our future is brighter than yours

Translated from the Zulu original – Bukelani Mmelly Shangase's Izizukulwane – by Dr Innocentia Jabulisile Mhlambi

INDULI YEXHWAYELO

IsiXhosa

Induli yaseMarikana; induli yexhwayelo
Apho kwahl'inyhikityha yokufa kwabembi zimbiwa
Bezomba phants' emathunjini omhlaba.

Imizimba yamaxhoba neengxwelerha;
yantyumpantyumpeka kwebomvu imbola
isezela elembol' ebomvu ivumba.

Imizimba izimbobo ngembobo zimbumbulu
zitaka kwintunjana, kwintanda yezandla zamaPolisa
kaRhulumente wentando yesininzi.

Unobangela ziintshukumo zezikhalazo
Kukhalazelwa unyuselo mvuzo ngabasebenzi
Loo ntshukumo yamitha yazala: Iingxwelerha,
    abahlolokazi,
Iinkedama, imiz' engenamadoda, abantwan' abaswel'
    oYise,
Kunye neentsaph' eziswel' abondli.

Funqu! umthamo kwizibhedlela ngenxa yeengxwelerha
Yakukuxakeka kubongi, abongikazi nooGqirha;
Kusindiswa ubomi bezo ngxwelerha,
Zimbi ziqatyulwa kwingqaqambo ezimandla
Zimbi zaphulukana nobomi kwintaba yexhwayelo.

Yaba lukrozo lwezithuthi;
zijonga ngomva amakhaya ngokwentsebenzo
zijongise amabombo kwawokuzalwa amakhaya
Ezinye zisinda-sindeka zizidumbu

Zimbi zisinda-sindeka ngabembi mgodi
benxunguphele emphefumlweni, besopha iintliziyo
bambi bentliziyo zinamahlwili kukuthinjelwa oogxa babo
   kukufa.

Emakhaya; yanda imihlambi yamangcwaba.
Noxa sele amila ingca loo mangcwaba nje!
Kwiintsapho ezohlulwe nezihlobo zazo
oku kosana olulele lulila isingqala asinasiqabu.

                SIWAPHIWE FORTUNE SHWENI

THE HILL OF AGONY

The Marikana Hill of agony,
Where miners died brutally.
They had to work underground.
Bodies of victims and casualties,
Died in pools of the so-called ochre.

While miners were sniffing blood,
Their bodies had bullet holes.
Bullets were from the Police hands.
Police of our Democratic Government.
Miners were complaining, that's the cause!

Armed miners decided to demonstrate and protest,
Demanded living wages and increase from their
  employers.
Miners' deaths, poor widows, appalled citizens!
Fatherless orphans, hunger, struggling families,
Those were the Marikana Hill consequences!

The Health civil servants moved up and down,
Did their best to save casualties, but we lost others.
From gunshots other miners died instantly.
Sprawled bodies filled the Marikana Hill.
The unforgettable scene of agony!

Affected families had to transport bodies,
From Marikana to the homes of the deceased.
Heartbroken citizens buried their breadwinners,
While other miners returned being disabled.
The sting of death caused so much pain!

Cemeteries had additional unexpected graves!
Heads of families were butchered ruthlessly.
Their families were left groaning with pain.
Graves without tombstones are covered with grass.
But the martyrs underground cannot be forgotten!

Translated from the Xhosa original – Siwaphiwe Fortune Shweni's Induli Yexhwayelo – by Angelinah Dazela

ANINA

ENGLISH

[1]I enjoyed the feeling
of rubbing my body against
anything I could
the thick lip of the bathtub
with no one in the house
cupboard doors
corner of beds sometimes
my hands

I wanted to rub myself against
something moving
so I brought one boy
home from school
It wasn't the first time
All the boys knew

That woman came home
from work early and
I was on top of him
he pushed me off
covered himself ran out
saying, Sorry, Auntie! Sorry!
I couldn't help but laugh

She caught me, dragged me
to the stove screaming
and switching both plates on
Her length of beautiful hair
swung close enough for me
to pull if my hands weren't

on the plates, my palms sizzled

Later she told me
I was disgusting
I was a filthy girl
No wonder you killed your mother
Then she came to me with
the butter for my hands

²I heard parts of what she said to my father,
I don't know what's wrong with that girl…
you must punish her for this…
she must calm down now…
you must take her out from school…
she's a filthy, ungrateful child…
she must get a job in a factory…
what will the neighbours say?
I only heard my father say,
When she was small,
I always found her with her hand down there

FRANCINE SIMON

DEEPA

English

Neela, I come down on you
                                      your legs separate mine
you tell me you are good at waiting
                                      my hips give way to your tongue
reaches in my mouth of ancestors
                                      the mouth of cousin-sisters
your hand comes around my trunk
                                      cut the first lips of my gurhal

Neela, you bend my skull
I will lick yours
I must say if I don't want
our vulvae bear and bear
jalebi wet

for feast

lick up my kantha here
Please!
you tell me
what you ask me to do
and bear until
we must leave this
crematorium
to wait

FRANCINE SIMON

NTWA YA BANA BA THARI

SETSWANA

Bana ba motho baalwana
Ba jana ka dinatha magobe
Bana ba kgwale ba tlhoka go bitsana ka melodi
Ke mpelegolole ke go lae
Ya re botlhogo putswa ba bua ba re
Ka tlhagolela mooka
Ya re o gola wa ntlhaba

Bontsi bo shebile dimpa
Ba lelwa ditilo go ja ka dimpa tse pedi
E re ditletse ba tlatse marama
Fa lemme le le mo bojeleng
Ba tlhoke go lekgaoganya
Jaaka tlhogo ya tsie
Yo monnye le yo mogolo
Ba tlhoke letswalo
Mme ba bolaye yo mongwe ntlheng ya bogagapa
Go tsaya lemme ele go ikhumisa
Ntswa khumo le lehuma di lala mmogo

Bana ba motho ba lwana
Moopedi fa a opela a re
Tlogela bana ba motho ba lwane
Bangwe ba tle batimi batlhoki tshono
Mme batlhoki ba tlhokele ruri

Ka khumo ele segwagwa e pharuma
E re e pharumile o ba tshwantse
Ba polotika fa go batliwa ditshwanelo tsa botho
Ba bua polotiki
Balwani ba ditshwanelo ba fetoge mapantiti

TIISETSO THIBA

CIVIL WAR

Siblings are fighting
Tearing at each other
Children of same parents, blood should be thicker than
    water
Let me tell you something
Seek wisdom from old generations
Keeping a snake warm didn't mean it wouldn't bite me

Many care only about their stomachs
It's an immense fight for hierarchy
More pockets are filling up
While you continue to drink to stupor
They divide and conquer
Old and new all the same
Have no fear no doubt
It's survival of the fittest
The weak must be eliminated
While the rich get richer

Brethren is fighting
When the singer sings and says
Let them fight it out
They must deny the poor a chance
And the poor remain destitute
While the rich reign supreme

The supremist will only come to enemy lines
To stand in the way of human rights endeavour
Talking politics
The freedom fighters are now prisoners

Translated from the Setswana original – Tiisetso Thiba's Ntwa Ya Bana Ba Thari – by Goodenough Mashego

FREEDOM

<small>ENGLISH</small>

leaves a window open
lifts the latch
lets itself out

Freedom travels across boundaries
passes dark hours, rides the tall wave
feels the furnace

Freedom pushes and struggles
cries and sheds blood
arrives different – new

Freedom waits, active and still
undoes and unwinds
looks behind and beyond

Freedom powers its own house
reaches and
holds unknown music

Freedom unfreezes its streams
looks afresh
at the face of another

Freedom broods, gives birth
in the blood of itself
is never alone

                ELIZABETH TREW

LIKE SILHOUETTES (AFTER FATHERLESS KIDS)

English

Silhouettes: the ever-present not so real people.
Always there
but not really even there.
That is what it is like to have a father
who was there
but not really even there; a silhouette.

When your father is a silhouette
you learn to embrace memories tightly until you suck the past out their bones

When your father is a silhouette
your mother masters the art of Sciography,
carefully constructing silhouettes that portray your father as a work of art,
leaving you to fill in the featureless voids of the skeleton

When your father is a silhouette
you learn that not all shadows belong to bodies
nor all bodies belong to their silhouettes

When your father is a silhouette
you ravage through the remnants of his footprints and shadow
keeping every bit and piece of his existence tucked under

your pillow
hoping that when you wake up
the tooth fairy will have swapped the silhouette for the
　　real thing

THATO TSHUKUDU

INNOCENT

AFRIKAANS

Sy toets haar oksels:
sy het nog haar slaaphemp aan
al het sy vroeg ver gestap.

Innocent sweet oor die pik:
hy grawe 'n fondasie
vir die raised gardens vir haar PermaCulture.

Sy sit op die stoep agter haar laptop,
maak vir hom tee,
herinner hom dat hy vloeistof moet inkry,

vir die son
(hy drink dit soet).

Die son vat lank om bo te kom.
Dit bly voormiddag.

Hy hou van sy spiere
waarvoor hy geoefen het:
'n ysterpaal
met twee sement gewigte
in 3-liter verfblikke gevorm.

Sy dink
hy droom oor Johannesburg
terwyl hy bou en grawe en bosse uitkap.

Iets byt haar –
sy is geskok

oor die wit vet wat bokant die denim hang
waar sy die bosluis aftrek.

Dit bly jeuk
die hele warm dag.

                ELNA VAN NIEKERK

INNOCENT

She checks her armpits:
she's still wearing her pyjama top
despite going for a long, early stroll.

Innocent sweats over the pick:
he's digging a foundation
for the raised gardens for her PermaCulture.

She sits on the stoep behind her laptop,
makes him some tea
reminds him to take enough fluids,

for the sun
(he drinks it sweet).

The sun takes its time to rise.
It remains morning.

He likes his muscles
for which he trained:
an iron pole
with two cement weights
formed in 3-litre paint cans.

She thinks
he's dreaming about Johannesburg
while he's building and digging and felling bushes.

Something bites her –
she's shocked

by the white fat hanging over the denim
where she removes the tick.

It keeps on itching
the whole hot day.

*Translated from the Afrikaans original – Elna van Niekerk's
Innocent – by Pieter Odendaal*

BELHAR

Afrikaans

ek is saam met die mense van Belhar
by 'n stakeholder feedback session
van die Safe Choices 4 Youth projek

sulke goed begin laat

uiteindelik het ek ook klaar gepraat
maar hulle vra my om die vote of thanks te doen
heel aan die einde
so ek moet nog konsentreer

voor die tyd het ek twee witmense gevra
waar is Bellville South se gemeenskapsaal:
hulle het my verkeerd verduidelik
en die Garmin het ook nie geweet nie

langs my sit 'n tannie:
sy's netjies aangetrek maar sy lyk bietjie verward
soos my ma
as sy nie mooi hoor wat gebeur nie

ek wonder wie vanoggend haar oorbelletjies ingehaak het

die International Funders
weet nie presies wat hulle will sien nie,
sit met beton smiles
en kyk na die rou talent
van die teenagers van Belhar:
gerapte boodskappe in gemengde Afrikaans
(vir hulle verlore)

agter die handjies
wat kruis oor die kruis
en amper dáár vat

jy wonder wat hulle dink maar gee vandag nie om nie

jy is deel daarvan

dis warm en mense stem nie saam nie
en mense wat jy uitgenooi het kom nie
en ander wat jy gehoop het
kom nie
is nou daar
en iemand het nie die brief verstaan nie
en nie alles vloei inmekaar nie

nie alles werk mooi uit nie

die program herkonstrueer rondom die wat daar is
(in plaas van die MEC en die burgemeester
het ons die CPF en die Neighbourhoodwatch)

Dan the Floor Killer vat die vloer

nou en dan kyk die tannie na my vir 'n cue
oor hoe sy moet reageer
maar ek is 'n gas
en ek is wit

en sy is nie seker of my gedrag
wel appropriate to the occasion is nie
die drama kinders skree in die mikrofoon
en dit laat die ou mense verbouereerd rondkyk:
wat gebeur nou?
hulle lag saam
sonder dat hulle verstaan

na middagete
wat genoeg is en betyds

(met die soort events weet mens nie altyd nie)

verlaat 'n paar mense die saal.

die tannie wat my aan my ma laat dink
groet my met 'n drukkie en sê
sy's bly ons het ontmoet,

sy gaan nou huis toe loop.

ELNA VAN NIEKERK

BELHAR

I'm joining the people of Belhar
at a stakeholder feedback session
for the Safe Choices 4 Youth project

these things start late

eventually I'm also done talking
but they ask me to do the vote of thanks
right at the end
so I still need to concentrate

beforehand I asked two white people
where Bellville South's community hall was;
they misdirected me
and the Garmin also didn't know

a lady is seated next to me:
she's neatly dressed but looks a bit perplexed
like my mom
when she can't quite hear what's going on

I wonder who put in her earrings today

the International Funders
don't exactly know what they want to see,
they sit with concrete smiles
and stare at the raw talent
of Belhar's teenagers:
rapped messages in mixed Afrikaans
(lost to them)

behind the hands
that cross the cross
and almost meet there

you wonder what they're thinking but you don't care
 today

you are part of it

it's hot and the people are disagreeing
and people that you invited didn't pitch
and others who you hoped
wouldn't come
are there now
and someone didn't understand the brief
and not everything is flowing smoothly

not everything is working out

the programme reconstructs around those who are there
(instead of the MEC and mayor
we have the CPF and the Neighbourhood watch)

Dan the Floor Killer takes to the floor

now and then the lady looks at me for a cue
as to how she should react
but I am a guest
and I am white
and she doesn't know if my behaviour

is in fact appropriate to the occasion

the drama kids shout into the microphone
the older people look around flustered:
what's happening now?
they laugh along
without understanding

after lunch
which is enough and on time
(with these kinds of events one doesn't always know)
a few people leave the hall.

that lady who reminds me of my mother
greets me with a hug and says
she's glad we met,

she's walking home now.

*Translated from the Afrikaans original – Elna van Niekerk's Belhar
– by Pieter Odendaal*

DIE OVERALL VAN MY

AFRIKAANS

'k staan op
vat 'n skoon hemp
uit die kas.
Trek hom aan ma
hy passie so lekker nie:
die collar is te styf
die moue te lank.

Gan Woolworths
toe vir hulle vaal, netjiese skool
broeke ma
dis te styf hie ommie hol;
vir kort bene
issie pype te lank.

Huur 'n suit vir my Matriek-afskeid,
so 'n blinke soos 'n krismislint.
Mos die blinkste is die stylish-ste.
Behalwe dis te styf hie ommie hol
te nou hie
en te wyd daa.

Wêk in 'n kantoor daa innie Kaap.
Stres oorrie regte skoene
en huil amper
wannie donnerse klere in allie donnerse winkels passie.
Viloorrie job ôk
wat fine is.

Kry 'n paint job op die plaas
lê lank leeg by die huis
– Willie Werker –
en Pa was ook 'n painter.
Die mense wonne sieke al lank al
wanneer my hoogmoed gan val
en ek in Pa se voetspore sal volg.

'k sit af Ko-Op
toe en krap deur die rakke
vir 'n wit overall
en pas hom an.
Die donnerse ding sit toe reg
hie ommie hol, ommie bene,
alles.
Die donnerse ding pas my
soos 'n handskoen.

        LESTER WALBRUGH

THIS OVERALL OF MINE

I get up
take a clean shirt
from the closet.
Put it on but
it doesn't quite fit:
the collar is too tight
the sleeves too long.

Off to Woolworths
for their grey, neat school
pants but
they're too tight here around the ass;
the legs are too long
for short limbs.

Hire a suit for my Matric farewell,
shiny like a Christmas ribbon.
The shinier, the fleeker, right?
Except it's too tight here around the ass
too narrow here
and too wide there.

Work in an office there in the Cape.
Stress about the right shoes
and almost cry
'coz the bloody clothes in all the bloody stores don't fit
Lose the job too
which is fine.

Get a paint job on the farm
Been idling my time away at home
– Willie Werker –
and Dad was a painter too.
People have probably been wondering
when my pride would come to a fall
and I would follow in Dad's footsteps.

I'm off to Co-Op
and rummage through the shelves
for a white overall
and try it on.
The bloody thing hugs me just fine
here around the ass, around the legs,
everything.
The bloody thing fits me
like a glove.

Translated from the Afrikaans original – Lester Walbrugh's Die Overall Van My – by Pieter Odendaal

CITY DUMP

ENGLISH

The cold nights are coming in
and those who have no home
other than the municipal dump,
are lighting fires in paint tins
to fall asleep in the tiny warmth.

When it jumps to brush and grass
the town wakes to acrid smoke,
hanging like guilt in the air.

JEANNIE WALLACE MCKEOWN

ACCUMULATED GRIEF

                                                                        ENGLISH

In the four months
since my mother died
I have been to five funerals.

At each one I mourn
more than the person
whose name
is on the leaflet.

       CRYSTAL WARREN

DETAILS OF DEATH

ENGLISH

At the dentist
for the first time
after your funeral
I realise
I need to change
the next of kin.

Crossing out your name
would be hard enough,
but the records are in pencil
and I am handed a rubber
to erase you from my file,
from my life.

    CRYSTAL WARREN

STATE OF THE NATION

English

I go to the pharmacy
to fill my prescription,
collect another month
of my chronic medication.

They tell me they are out of stock
of two of the tablets.
They can help my cholesterol
but the high blood pressure tablets
and antidepressants
are sold out.

They give me a few tablets
to tide me over,
from a precious store
sourced from other
chemists in town,
who are also low on supplies.
They promise to deliver
as soon as the new stock arrives.

I am not sure
if I should be relieved
that I am not alone
in my affliction,
or concerned

that so many people
in this small city
are also
stressed and depressed.

   CRYSTAL WARREN

IMMIGRANT

ENGLISH

salty breezes call to my senses.
I awake to the Spanish sun
teasing the horizon, the
ocean giggles and glistens.

fruits and cheese and wine
lay spread for morning feasts;
the pavements singing
sizzling songs of decadence.

matadors parade their crisp attire
as we stroll through the cobled square.
a bandurria's melody recalls
an elderly couple's youthful love.

and the creeking door of my tin shack
reminds me, home remains a memory.

                FLOW WELLINGTON

APOLLONIAN TRICK

ENGLISH

The sombre display draws a crowd to the square –
a shuffle of ashen young men clothed in chains
red-brown with time, heavy with memory. In turn

they shed their dress onto a mountainous pile, coiled,
hissing in the low sun. With shining faces the men
skip away in white rags and Phrygian caps. But

as soon as they leave, their shackles grow back.
The puzzled crowd thins as one last man appears, too
shuffling under metal restraints. He labours to cast

his demons to the tangled beast. Unlike those before,
he struts away, forever without chains, having traded
white rag and cap, for black robe and mortarboard.

ATHOL WILLIAMS

BIOGRAPHIES

Zukiswa Muriel Adonis is a 42-year-old food technologist who loves arts and culture, i.e. listening to and reading poetry (Xhosa and English), reading Xhosa and English novels, watching drama/theatre performances (Xhosa, English and a bit of Afrikaans). Baxter and Artscape are her second homes. She loves travelling (locally and internationally) and visiting museums (for their sculptures and photographs). She enjoys window shopping for clothes and ornaments in flea markets and writes Xhosa poems as a hobby.

Jim Pascual Agustin was born in Marikina, the shoemaking industry capital of the Philippines. He lives on the fringes of Cape Town with his lovely wife and twin daughters, along with an ageing dog and a stray cat that decided to stay. He has published poetry collections in Filipino and English since 1992. His work has appeared in *Rhino, World Literature Today, Modern Poetry in Translation, New Coin, Aerodrome and New Contrast among others*. His latest poetry collection, *How to Make a Salagubang Helicopter*, is due to be released by San Anselmo Publications in 2018. Agustin also writes a blog (www.matangmanok.wordpress.com).

Du Toit Albertze is a theatre-maker, scriptwriter and poet. He is currently working on his BA honours degree in theatre directing at Stellenbosch University. Some of his theatre work includes: *Bos, Vaselinetjie, Die Reëngodin, Kommapunt, Steriel, (W)asem* and *Die Meermin Kompleks*. As a spoken word poet he has been part of the Inzync Poetry Collection team for more than three years. He is an artist who strongly supports queer, feminist and mental health issues and believes strongly in the breaking down of destructive Afrikaner structures.

Kyle Allan is a writer, recording artist and event organiser. He has published two books of poetry, *House without walls* (2016) and *The space between us* (2018), and has released one album, *Influences* (2013).

Mia Arderne is a writer, columnist and poet from Cape Town. She performed at the McGregor Poetry Festival in 2017 and was published in the *Sol Plaatje European Union Poetry Anthology* in 2013. She completed her MA in English creative writing at UCT after receiving the NRF Freestanding Masters scholarship. Her columns have been published by *Marie Claire*, *City Press*, *GQ* magazine and *Matador Network* among others. Her short stories have appeared in various anthologies and her debut novel was short-listed for the Dinaane Debut Fiction Award. Her writing explores themes of identity, marginalisation and sexuality.

Vonani Bila is the author of five books of poems in English and eight storybooks for newly literate adult readers in Xitsonga, Sepedi and English. Bila is a driving force in South African poetry as the founding editor of the *Timbila* poetry journal, publisher of Timbila books and founder of Timbila Writers' Village, a rural retreat centre for writers. He teaches in the Department of English Studies at the University of Limpopo.

René Bohnen is an Afrikaans poet who was born and bred in KZN. She now lives in Johannesburg and in the Western Cape, working as a freelance writer, translator and photographer. She holds a master's degree in Creative

Writing and has published three books of poetry, *Spoorsny* (2000), *in die niks al om* (2011) and *Op die vingerpunte van die heelal* (2017).

Christine Coates is a poet and writer from Cape Town. She has an MA in creative writing from the University of Cape Town. Her poems and stories have been published in various literary journals. Her debut collection, *Homegrown*, published in 2014 by Modjaji Books, received an honourable mention from the Glenna Luschei Prize. Her second collection will be published later in 2018. Her poems have been selected for the *Sol Plaatje European Union Poetry* anthologies every year since inception: 2011–2017, and *Best "New" African Poets* 2015 and 2016 anthologies.

Silulundi Coki ngumfundi owenza unyaka wesithathu kwiDyunisithi yaseKapa (University of Cape Town). Uyaluthanda ulwimi de esikolweni ufunda Isixhosa, Isingesi kunye neSociology. Uzibona engumbhali owaziwa jikelele, ebhala ngelwimi lenkobe isiXhosa kutsho. Masibuyeleni embo.

Mark de Wet is a published author living in KZN. He is hoping to publish two books this year, one of which is a 'visual fusion of wine and poetry' and is 150 verses long, based on the *Rubaiyat of Omar Khayham*, written a thousand years ago. Poetry has always been one of his 'secret loves'.

Luthando Dlamini was born in Margate, KwaZulu-Natal. He is an LLB student at the University of Cape Town.

Ruth Everson is a poet, writer and speaker who uses her

work to encourage, inspire and inquire. She has presented lectures and workshops on poetry and creativity at festivals, schools, conferences and gatherings across South Africa. Her poetry has taken her to China, Egypt, Lesotho, Swaziland and Botswana. For her, to quote one of her poems: "Poetry is dangerous, Poetry will write your tears in ink, Poetry will hang your soul on barbed wire lines."

Nobuntu Gantana is a lover of all forms of art. Her fascination with languages is what fuelled her passion in writing. She is currently based in Grahamstown where she is studying part-time and working as a government official. In her personal capacity she mentors young girls on life-skills. Her writing explores various social issues affecting women in society. One of her poems was published in Volume VI of the *Sol Plaatje European Union Poetry Anthology* in 2016. Her second poem 'Dadobawo ndicel' amandla' was published in Volume VII of the same poetry anthology in 2017.

Sarah Godsell was born in 1985, in Johannesburg, South Africa. She is a historian and poet. She began performing in 2009 and has performed nationally and internationally on various stages, radio and TV platforms. She has been published in journals such as *Poetry Potion*, *New Coin*, *Astra* and *Illuminations*, and her words appear in edited collections such as *Home is Where the Mic is* and *Marikana: A Moment in Time*. Her first collection, *Seaweed Sky*, came out in 2016, and was a finalist for the HSS Fiction Awards in 2018.

Richard Higgs is a lecturer in digital curation at the University of Cape Town. He holds master's degrees in language sciences and creative writing. He was born in

Boksburg and is a keen amateur actor and director, as well as an activist for autism.

Veronique Jephtas is a 21-year-old final-year drama and theatre studies student at Stellenbosch University. She is specialising in directing and voice art. Jephtas is a firm believer in the fact that she cannot do everything, but what she can do she can do very good. Her goal is to be a storyteller. She wants and loves to go to places in her stories where others are too scared to go. Her passion lies in performing and writing. She always strives to not only learn, but to learn to apply, to listen, to be.

Zandile Khumalo is a 31-year-old new writer, born and bred in Mariannhill outside of Durban. Molle is an aspiring novelist who is currently working on her debut fantasy/adventure novel. Her poem 'Ngenze Nami Ngizigqaje' is a young girl's yearning for a soulmate.

Thabiso Tsietsi Lakajoe ke mongodi wa dithothokiso Sesotho. Lakajoe ke mongodi ya lwanelang setso le ditokelo tsa puo ya letswele hore le yona e tshwane e hlokomelwe jwaloka puo tse ding. Tse ding tsa dithothokiso tsa hae di phatlaladitswe ho *ITCH* journal, *Poetry Potion*, AvBob Poetry Competition, *Love Letters to My Child*, 2015, 2016 & 2017 *Sol Plaatjie European Union Poetry Anthology*.

George Thabiso Leseba is a University of the Free State student, poet, writer and motivator. He is very passionate about mother tongue and is not afraid to express his feelings through it. He is a winner of the regional Ubuntu competitions for kids' radio, and he represented QwaQwa Radio on a national level with his Sotho essay that came in second place and left many people craving more.

Busisiwe Mahlangu is a writer, perfomer and TEDx speaker. She is the founder of Lwazilubanzi, a community-based project aimed at using literature as a tool of resistance and healing. She has performed her work around South Africa, including Open Book Festival (CPT), Words In My Mouth Slam Week (Mpumalanga) and the Vavasati International Women's Festival. Her poetry was longlisted for the Sol Plaatje European Union Poetry Award in 2017.

Tshepiso Makgoloane is a 21-year-old visionary who was raised in a village called Patantshwane at Sekhukhune district. She later moved to Motetema where she currently resides. She has aspired to write in both Sepedi and English since 2014 when she was still in high school and she is currently a committed LLB student at the University of South Africa.

Mbali Malimela is a strictly isiZulu female writer and perfomer from KZN. She has showcased some of her work on the national radio station UKhozi.fm. She has also perfomed on different stages around Durban, like The Bat Centre, Playhouse Theatre (Sundowners) and the Durban Poetry Show (DPS), as well as in Cape Town, at the Baxter Theatre & Obviouzly Armchair.

Anga Mamfanya is a spoken word artist based in Pretoria. He made his performance debut in 2016 at the Tshwane Speak Out Loud Youth Poetry Competition, in which he was the 2nd prize winner. He has shared his original work at the University of Johannesburg and the University of Pretoria as a guest speaker. Mamfanya is the founder of

Blvcksuburbia, a social movement that aims to empower black communities through poetry and art.

Sibulelo Manamatela is a literature student and poet based in Johannesburg. She is a great lover of any worthwhile written text whether it is in novels, plays, music or poetry. Perhaps it is language that she is really in love with.

Tshedza Mashamba is a 17-year-old South African black female currently doing her matric year at Hyde Park High School. She began writing in 2015 and is a published author of three poems and one short story.

Bongani Masilela is a native of South Africa born in 1992. He is a mathematician, poet and a human rights activist who was born with a physical disability. Masilela has authored a poetry anthology titled *Then I don't want to be a Poet*. Despite him having studied mathematics, his love for art and sport is massive.

Aaron Mpho Masowa is an author and analyst of Sesotho books, and a teacher. He has currently published four books. Namely *Jo, bophelo bona!*, *Lenyora* and *Dikakata tsa bophel*. He is currently pursuing a PhD with the University of the Free State.

Zongezile Matshoba can be found wherever there is a literary event for the young and old. His writings narrate the humour and hardships of township and rural life and interrogate whether it is yet uhuru in people's livelihood.

Katise Mawela is a Johannesburg-based award-winning poet and cultural activist. His poems have appeared in various publications including *Tribute* magazine. He is also a freelance journalist.

Marthe McLoud is 'n maatskaplike werker en woon in die Strand. Verskeie van haar gedigte en kortverhale is op Litnet gepubliseer. In 2017 was sy een van die *Nuwe Stemme 6* wat deur Tafelberg uitgegee is, waarin ses van haar gedigte gepubliseer is. Van haar gedigte het ook in 2018 in die *New Contast Literary Journal* verskyn.

Janine Milne holds a bachelor's degree in theory of literature and creative writing, with distinctions, from the University of South Africa. She won the McGregor Poetry Festival poetry competition and had several poems published in *The Sol Plaatje European Union Poetry Anthology* Volume IV. Her short stories were chosen for the coveted *Short Sharp Stories Anthology*, *Die Laughing* and *The Bloody Parchment*, the 2016 South African Horror Festival anthology. She is currently working on her first poetry collection and novel.

Thabiso Mofokeng started writing at the age of 15. He is a versatile writer – writing in Sesotho and English. Some of his Sesotho books are prescribed by the Department of Education for Grade 8 and Grade 10. After working as a self-made Sesotho language practitioner, he found himself becoming the founding publisher of Mosa Media and Book Distributors (Pty) Ltd – excelling in publishing books written in African languages. Thabiso completed his Master of Arts in creative writing with distinctions at Rhodes University in 2015. He is currently studying a PhD in English at the University of the Western Cape. He is a 2016/17 Dinaane Debut Fiction Award Finalist. He was named as one of the *Mail and Guardian* #200 Young South Africans 2017. His latest novel is *The Last Stop*.

Daniel Matsepe Mohlala is a 27-year-old BCom graduate (University of Limpopo) from the rural village of Moeding, on the outskirts of Marble Hall. A poet who aspires to write in Sepedi, his love for literature began when he was in high school. In April 2018 he co-authored a book titled *Broken Dreams: The Awakening Past* with Edwin D Mabodimo Mphaga. He previously served as a freelance translator for *Sekhukhune Times* newspaper. He currently lives in Motetema. He has a daughter named Bohlale.

Dikeledi Mokoena is a black woman born in Sebokeng, a township in South Africa. She is a PhD candidate in political science and lectures African feminism and gender studies at the Thabo Mbeki African Leadership Institute. She identifies with some 'isms' such as pan-Africanism and African feminism. She is a lover of laughter and life and reveres God and her ancestors.

Mjele Msimang is a Tshwane-based poet, fiction writer and educator. He began writing in 2016 as a way of self-exploration and self-awareness. His work is highly influenced by rap, hiphop and history. He has guest lectured history through poetry at the universities of the Witwatersrand and Johannesburg and has performed on various stages in and around Johannesburg and Tshwane. His poems seek to explore himself and his surroundings, speaking to structural inequality, personal triumphs and loss, family, love, sexuality, culture and traditions. He hopes that through his writing he can add to the voices battling for a brighter, more inclusive future and history.

Moses Mtileni is the author of *Mpimavayeni* (a novel), *Nhlalala* (a novel) and *U Ya Va Rungula* (poetry). He has curated a Xitsonga poetry anthology, *Ntsena loko Mpfula A Yo Sewula*, and has translated the works of, among others, Peter Horn and Ngũgĩ wa Thiong'o into Xitsonga. His poetry has appeared in a few volumes of the *Sol Plaatje European Union Poetry Anthology*, *Illuminations*, *Asymptote*, *Timbila*, *Botsotso*, and *Poetry Potion*. He comes from Nkuri-Tomu Village in Limpopo.

Sifiso Mtshali was raised and educated in Daveyton. He is an aspiring poet and an upcoming writer. He has been shortlisted twice in the SA Writers College short story competition. Mtshali is passionate about all things classical, from paintings to literature, he is a lover of words and the power they wield.

Sinaso Mxakaza is a young South African writer who started writing in 2008 inspired by her love for books. Her poems are about healing, change and finding one's voice in the world we live in. Her work has been published online on sites such as VoicesNet, Fundza and in online anthologies like *Poetry Potion* and *Next Generation Speaks Global Youth Anthology*.

Pamela Newham is a journalist, author of children's books and a poet. She runs workshops on journalism and writing books for children. She lives in Cape Town. Her poems have been published in anthologies and literary journals. Her poetry collection, *Washing Day in the Bush*, was published in 2017.

Sandile Ngidi is a poet, translator, freelance journalist and dramatist. He was born in Vryheid in 1969 and grew up in Amahlongwa on the south coast of Durban. He is the Zulu-to-English translator of Sibusiso Nyembezi's classic Zulu novel, *Inkinsela yaseMgungundlovu*. He is currently an MA creative writing student at Rhodes University.

Bomikazi Njoloza is a versatile writer, poet and advocate for mother-tongue literacy; a child and student of the universe. She arrived on this planet over two decades ago in the land of silent hills, iminga and scarlet aloes. This daughter of forgiveness moulds poetry; speaks and tells stories in more ways than we have found a language for. As Zakes Mda said in a foreword to her debut anthology, 'hers is a voice that demands to be heard'. Njoloza's debut poetry anthology, *The Colour of Love*, was published in 2012 and she has since published extensively in isiXhosa, English and German.

Simphiwe Nolutshungu is a published poet and writer. Last year he won a SALA award in poetry. He holds a master's degree in creative writing and is a teacher by qualification. He works as a lecturer at the University of Cape Town, in the Department of African Languages and Literature, and is currently pursuing his PhD in IsiXhosa.

Zola Nongogo was born in the Eastern Cape in Mount Ayliff and currently lives in Cape Town. He has been published in *Prufrock* magazine, *The Sol Plaatje European Union Poetry Anthology* in 2015 and 2017 and the online literary journal *Eunoia Review* under the name Zukisani Nongogo.

USipho Albert Ntombela wazalelwa eMnambithi

eMatiwaneskop kwesenkosi uShabalala nokuyilapha afunda khona imfundo yamabanga aphansi.Waqala ukufunda eCwembe BC School wase edlulela eMangcengeza Secondary School wagcina ephothule ibanga leshumi Emhlwaneni High School. Waqhubeka wafundela ubuthisha eBethel College of Education kusuka ngonyaka we-1988 kuya kowe-1990. Ngonyaka we-1991 waqala ukufundisa eQhudeni Public School eNkandla. Ezinye izikole aseke wafundisa kuzo UMgazi Public School, Lerato-uThando High School kanye Heritage Combined School. Useke waba yiNhloko yeziLimi ezikolweni ezehlukene, ibamba likaThishanhloko, uThisha-nhloko kanye noMeluleki wezikolo olimini lwesiZulu. Ngesikhathi efundisa ubefunda ngasese e-Unisa waze waphothula iziqu zobudokotela. Ngonyaka we-2012 waqala ukufundisa eWits School of Education nokuyilapho enguMphathi welimi zabampisholo.

Mushayathoni Bridget Nwovhe is a medical student and the author of a book titled *Calendar's Time*. She's also an editor at her recently found publishing company (Yoanda Khano Publishing), a speaker and a mentor to many. She has been featured in many different newspapers, like *Limpopo Mirror*, and has been interviewed on radio stations like Phalaphala FM. She believes in healing through poetry and medicine, which is maybe why she's doing both.

Hans Pienaar has published two collections of poetry (*Die Taal van Voëls*, *Notas uit die Empire*) in Afrikaans and one of photo-poems (*Uithoeke/Outcorners*). He is a former chair of the Melville Poetry Festival. He has also written three works of fiction and written and produced several plays. He won the Pansa national award for *Three Dozen Roses*, the Marius Jooste Prize for his MA in creative writing (cum laude), the Rapport Prize for Non-Fiction and the Cosaw Prize for short stories. His poems and stories have been anthologised in various collections.

Sehloho Piet Rampai was born in 1985 and has a law degree from NMMU. He has published regularly with *Poetry Potion*.

Juliette Rose-Innes is a 19-year-old Capetonian living in Woodstock. She was a finalist for the Scribe Scriptwriting Competition (2017) and has been published in *English Alive* (2016 and 2017). She currently attends the University of Cape Town and is studying a degree in theatre and performance, aspiring to write and direct plays. Her favourite writers include Kurt Vonnegut, John Irving, Samuel Beckett and Emily Berry. Along with writing, she enjoys reading, photography and wearing unfashionable clothes.

Deborah Seddon is a poet, feminist and academic. She was born and raised in Harare, Zimbabwe. She has lived and worked in Grahamstown, in the Eastern Cape, for a long time. She teaches poetry, Early Modern Literature, African-American, African, and Afro-Caribbean literature at USKAR, the University Still Known as Rhodes. Her current research focuses on South African and African-American spoken word, and on queer literature and film.

Moses Seletisha is a radical performance poet, translator and author of *Tšhutšhumakgala* (his first published title). He is a native writer who hails from the deep rural areas of Ga-Matlala 'a Rakgwadi (Tsimanyane village), not far from Marble Hall in the then Northern Province. An intellectual whose area of interest is African languages and their social context, Seletisha has chosen to restrict himself from writing in any language other than Sepedi. By any means necessary, Seletisha prides himself as having been circumcised by notable Sepedi writers such as Goodenough Mashego, Dr David Maahlamela, Matete Motsoaledi and more not mentioned. Some of his work has been featured in various forms of literary journals, that include the *Botsotso* poetry anthology and *megaArtists* magazine. He is the winner of the Sol Plaatje European Union Poetry Award 2017 and the winner of the South African Literary Award as First-time Published Author (2017). He was invited by the National Library of South Africa to perform a poem "Kgadime" – in celebration of OK Matsepe. Pula!

Nkwana Joshua Serutle is a writer, spoken word poet and fine artist, who was born and raised outside Burgersfort, Limpopo. In 2017 he joined Mzansi Poetry Academy to enhance his writing skills. His work draws much attention on the streets, shifting paradigms on social issues. Some of his highlights in 2017 included performing on SABC 1's, YoTV. Later on that year he became Top 10 finalist for Leleme La Mme poetry competition. Some of his work is published in *Poetry Potion* and *Odd Magazine*.

UBukelani Mmelly Shangase wazalwa wakhulela kwaMaphumulo KwaZulu-Natal. Ungowokuqala ezinganeni eziyisikhombisa zikaNyenyezile Shangase noMqiniseni Mali Shangase. Njengeningi labaculi walifulathela ikhaya weza eGoli ngonyaka we-1980, okunamanje usazinze khona. Usesebenze isikhathi eside endimeni yomculo womaskandi. Naba abanye babaculi balolu hlobo lomculo aseke wasebenza nabo: Umfaz' omnyaka Khumalo, Ikhansela noJBC, noFive

Roses Dlamini. Ngaphandle kokucula ukhonze ukubhala izinkondlo zesiZulu.

Siwaphiwe Fortune Shweni was born in 1995 in a small village in the Eastern Cape, Engcobo. He studied at Tshatshatsha PJS, Freemantle Boys' High School and Cape Peninsula University of Technology in the Western Cape. His work is published in *The Kalahari Review*, *Prufrock* issue 12 and on the Avbob poetry website (2017). He was one of the finalists in the 2016 McGregor poetry competition.

Francine Simon was born in 1990 in Durban to Indian Catholic parents. She recently completed her doctorate in English studies at Stellenbosch University. Her poems have been published in South African literary journals such as *New Coin* and *Aerodrome*. She launched her debut collection of poetry, *Thungachi*, in 2017. She is currently working on a new poetry project about South African Indian identity.

Tiisetso Thiba is a poet and novelist and was born in a village called Ganyesa in North West. He has written two books, a poetry book titled *Let's Take a Walk, Mama* (2015) and a Setswana novel titled *Tlhabane Ya Makgowa* (2017). Thiba has started to write more of his work in Setswana to promote and preserve his language. He has been on the SABC youth programme *Mzansi Insider* and was been featured on News24 and Beautiful News in 2017 for his Setswana book. Tiisetso is currently working as a communications officer.

Elizabeth Trew returned to South Africa in 1991 after decades out of the country. She has an MA in English education from Wits, facilitates writing workshops for

People Opposing Women Abuse (POWA) and volunteers at a shelter for girls in Cape Town. Her poems have appeared in various poetry journals in South Africa and England, a selection in *ISISx* (Botsotso) and *Prodigal Daughters: Stories of South African women in exile*, edited by Lauretta Ngcobo (UKZN Press).

Thato Tshukudu is the 2017 national winner of the Poetry in Mcgregor competition and is featured in the 2016 and 2017 *Best New African Poets Anthology*, Volume VIII of the *Sol Plaatje European Union Anthology, Better Than Starbucks, Poetry Potion*. Thato released his debut body of poetry titled *fly in a beehive* in 2018

Elna van Niekerk started her first job as a lecturer in philosophy at the University of the North, stayed on her own in the Wolkberg mountains for a few months, was a bus driver for the Tshwane City Council and then worked in Transport Safety research at the CSIR for 19 years. Currently she manages her own company. She has four children and lives in Pretoria. Recently some of her poems were accepted for publication in *Nuwe Stemme 6*.

Lester Walbrugh is from Grabouw in the Western Cape. He writes short fiction and poems and is an editorial member of Type/Cast, an online literary journal. His work has been published in the short story anthologies of the National Arts Festival and Short Story Day Africa.

Jeannie Wallace McKeown lives in Grahamstown, South Africa, and writes poetry and prose creatively. She works full-time at Rhodes University but also as a freelance writer covering academic lectures, seminars and book launches. She has had creative pieces published in literary journals and online, is the mother of two boys who can no longer be described as small and is in a steady co-parenting relationship with an ex-husband. Her collection, *Unremembered Poems*, will be published by Modjaji Books in 2018.

Crystal Warren grew up in Port Elizabeth but has lived and worked in Grahamstown for nearly 30 years. She has worked as a librarian, literary researcher and museum curator, and has always been surrounded by books. Her poems have appeared in several anthologies and journals. Her first collection, *Bodies of Glass*, appeared in 2004 and the long delayed second collection, *Predictive Text*, will come out in 2018.

Flow Wellington is the author of two self-published collections, *The Undelivered Score* and *Gau-Trained*. She is the founding owner of Poetree Publications, a company that offers African writers affordable publishing and distribution services. To date, the company has 15 titles under its belt. Flow has been published in local and international publications including *To Breathe Into Another Voice* (SA jazz anthology) and *The Atlanta Review*. She also acts as a curating consultant for the Eastern Cape Book Festival committee.

Athol Williams has published four poetry collections and his poems have been published in over 40 publications internationally. His creative and scholarly work focuses on identifying and eradicating structural barriers to social justice and celebrating humanity's great possibilities. Athol holds degrees from Oxford, Harvard, LSE, MIT, London Business School and Wits.

What is the European Union (EU)?

The European Union is a unique economic and political union between 28 European countries[1] that together cover much of the continent. The EU was created in the aftermath of the Second World War. The first steps were to foster economic cooperation: the idea being that countries that trade with one another become economically interdependent and so more likely to avoid conflict.

Since its birth, the union has developed into a huge single market with the euro as its common currency. What began as a purely economic union has evolved into an organisation spanning policy areas from climate, environment and health to external relations and security, justice and migration.

The single or 'internal' market is the EU's main economic engine, enabling most goods, services, money and people to move freely. Another key objective is to develop this huge resource also in other areas like energy, knowledge and capital markets to ensure that Europeans can draw the maximum benefit from it.

The EU is based on the rule of law: everything it does is founded on treaties, voluntarily and democratically agreed by its member countries. It actively promotes human rights and democracy and in 2012 was awarded the Nobel Peace Prize for advancing the causes of peace, reconciliation, democracy and human rights in Europe.

How does it work?
EU Member States have set up institutions to run the EU and adopt its legislation. The main ones are:
- The European Parliament (representing the people of

Europe)
- The Council of the European Union (representing national governments)
- The European Commission (representing the common EU interest)

Size & population
The EU is less than half the size of the United States covering some 4 million km². In terms of size, France is the EU's largest country and Malta its smallest. The EU has a population of close to 505 million people – the world's third largest after China and India.

The EU's economy
Operating as a single market, the EU is a major world trading power. EU economic policy seeks to sustain growth by investing in transport, energy and research while minimising the impact of further economic development on the environment. Measured in terms of the goods and services it produces, its economy is bigger than that of the US.

EU symbols
- The European flag – The 12 stars in a circle symbolise the ideals of unity, solidarity and harmony among the peoples of Europe.
- The European anthem – The melody used to symbolise the EU comes from Ludwig Van Beethoven's 9th Symphony composed in 1823.
- Europe Day – The ideas behind the EU were first put forward on 9 May 1950 by French Foreign Minister

Robert Schuman. This is why 9 May is celebrated as a key date for the EU.
- The EU motto – "United in diversity".

The EU & South Africa – a partnership of equals

Since 1994 the growing relationship between South Africa and the EU has been underpinned by the Trade, Development and Cooperation Agreement (TDCA). Closer ties between the two parties were consolidated in 2007 with the establishment of the EU-SA Strategic Partnership.

This partnership, the only one of its kind with an African country, is centred on enhanced political dialogue around issues of shared interest including climate change, the global economy, governance, bilateral trade, and peace and security matters. In line with this, its action plan encompasses sectoral cooperation on a range of issues such as climate change, environment, education, science and technology, space, trade and migration.

Regular high level meetings steer the partnership, along with the EU-South Africa Joint Cooperation Council. They provide the occasions to discuss current bilateral, regional and global issues.

Trade & investment

The EU is South Africa's most important trading partner. In 2017, according to Eurostat, the EU was the destination of some 22% (R262 bn) of total SA exports and the source of close to 30.5% (R338 bn) of total SA imports. Manufactured goods comprise a meaningful component of

SA's exports, with over half the exports to the EU leaving SA shores in processed or semi-processed form. EU countries are also the source of some 74% of foreign direct investment (FDI) stock in South Africa.

Development cooperation
The EU remains an important development partner to South Africa, providing significant external assistance funds. The EU's total indicative grant budget for South Africa for the period 2014–20 amounts to some €250 million. It is complemented by a €416 million loan finance envelope from the European Investment Bank (EIB) as well as grant funding from the EU Member States.

---

* Belgium, Bulgaria, Croatia, Czech Republic, Denmark, Germany, Estonia, Ireland, Greece, Spain, France, Italy, Cyprus, Latvia, Lithuania, Luxembourg, Hungary, Malta, the Netherlands, Austria, Poland, Portugal, Romania, Slovenia, Slovakia, Finland, Sweden, and the United Kingdom.